Learning Microsoft PRISM4 by Example

FLORIN BADEA

ALIN BADEA

Copyright © 2014 Florin Badea, Alin Badea

All rights reserved.

ISBN:1497436281
ISBN-13:978-1497436282

To our family

CONTENTS

Acknowledgements	i
Chapter 1: Initializing a PRISM Application	1
1.1 Initializing PRISM applications	1
1.2 Bootstrapper features	4
1.3 Custom bootstrappers	7
1.4 Custom logging	14
1.5 Summary	16
Chapter 2: Modular Applications	17
2.1 Modules	17
2.2 Module Catalogs	18
2.3 Module dependencies and initialization modes	21
2.4 Module Managers and Initializers	23
2.5 Building a modular application	24
2.6 Building a custom module type loader	30
2.6.1 Creating the WCF service	31
2.6.2 Building the WPF client	33
2.7 Summary	40
Chapter 3: The MVVM design pattern	41
3.1 MVVM components	41
3.2 MVVM Class interactions	42
3.3 Instantiating the view and view-model classes	43
3.4 Implementing an MVVM application	45
3.5 Summary	65
Chapter 4: User interaction	67

4.1 Using an interaction service	67
4.1.1 Testing with the interaction service	73
4.2 Using interaction request objects	75
4.2.1 Testing with interaction request objects	85
4.3 Summary	86 |//
Chapter 5: Inter module communications — 89
5.1 Composite Commands	89
5.2 Event Aggregators	103
5.3 Shared Services	107
5.4 Summary	109

Chapter 6: Regions — 111

6.1 Defining regions	111
6.2 View discovery	112
6.3 View injection	114
6.4 Building a region based application	115
6.5 Summary	137

Chapter 7: Region Navigation — 139

7.1 State-based navigation	139
7.2 View-based navigation	141
7.3 Summary	160

Chapter 8: Deploying PRISM applications — 161

8.1 Deploying Silverlight applications	161
8.2 Deploying WPF applications	164
8.2.1 Deploying WPF PRISM applications with ClickOnce	164
8.2.2 Deploying WPF PRISM applications with WindowsInstaller	167
8.2.3 Deploying WPF PRISM applications with WiX	171
8.3 Summary	173

References — 175

Appendix: The PRISM Framework — 177

Installing PRISM	177
PRISM assemblies	177
Source code	178
Quickstarts and reference implementations	178

ACKNOWLEDGMENTS

First of all, we would like to thank our family for being there for us every step of the way. The book to a long time to write and there were times when we were unsure of whether it will ever be finished. Our family always supported us and encouraged us to go on and we want to thank them for this. We would also like to thank Oana Scutariu for her work on designing and creating the book cover.

CHAPTER 1: INITIALIZING A PRISM APPLICATION

Implementing a composite application can be difficult at first. Some things need to be configured before showing the user interface (UI) and you need to commit to using some best practices in order to successfully develop the application in such a way that makes it easy to test, maintain and extend. You need to write your code in a loosely coupled fashion so that components can be easily replaced if necessary.

One proven way to write such code is to use dependency injection. Dependency injection represents a set of software design principles that allows you to write loosely coupled code. By using dependency injection, the class dependencies are injected instead of being hard coded. This way the class does not have to worry about how the dependency is created and how it works. At some point these dependencies still need to be instantiated and linked to the classes that use them. The place where this takes place is called the application composition root.

For small applications it's easy enough to create and assign these dependencies manually. This is not the case for complex applications that work with hundreds of classes. Other things need to be taken into account as well: object lifecycle management, object composition and interception. These are very difficult to implement properly. Fortunately there are specialized classes that handle these problems automatically. These classes are called dependency injection containers. They handle instance creation, object composition, object lifecycle management and interception.

Before building a PRISM application you need to decide what dependency injection (DI) container you want to use. You can choose the DI container based on your style or on application requirements. PRISM supports 2 DI containers out of the box: Unity and MEF. Choosing a DI container is important because it determines the type of bootstrapper you will use to initialize the composite application.

1.1 Initializing PRISM applications

Any PRISM application needs to run some initialization logic before showing the UI. This is because multiple PRISM services need to be set up for everything to work correctly. All this initialization code is contained in a central place called a bootstrapper. PRISM offers an abstract Bootstrapper class that needs to be implemented. PRISM also offers 2 implementations of this class out of the box. If you want to inject your dependencies by using the UnityContainer you should initialize your application by using a UnityBootstrapper instance. If you want to inject your dependencies with MEF you should use a MefBootstrapper instance.

If none of these containers work for you, you have the option of using a third party container or even your very own implementation. All you have to do is implement the abstract Bootstrapper class and the IServiceLocator interface. PRISM is container agnostic. This is achieved by using the service locator pattern. PRISM components use the IServiceLocator interface to resolve dependencies. The default implementation of the IServiceLocator interface delegates the responsibility of resolving services to a UnityContainer instance or to a CompositionContainer instance, depending on your choice (Unity or MEF respectively).

Both UnityBootstrapper and MefBootstrapper have a single abstract method, called CreateShell, which needs to be implemented. This method creates the Shell of the application. The Shell represents the application's main window or root visual. All application visual elements, or views, will be composed inside the Shell. Views will be supplied by different modules and will be registered to particular regions defined in the Shell. In order to initialize a PRISM application you need to at least provide the Shell. A basic implementation of a bootstrapper class can be seen in listing 1.1.

Listing 1.1 – *A bootstrapper implementation that uses the Unity DI container*
```
public class Bootstrapper:UnityBootstrapper
{
    protected override DependencyObject CreateShell()
    {
        return new MainPage();
    }
}
```

The bootstrapper class from listing 1.1 derives from the UnityBootstrapper class. This class uses the Unity DI container to handle dependencies between objects. In order to initialize an application with this bootstrapper we need to create a bootstrapper instance and call its Run method. For a Silverlight application this can be done in the event handler for the application's Startup event. The initialization code can be seen in listing 1.2.

Listing 1.2 – *Initializing the application by creating a bootstrapper and calling its Run method*
```
private void Application_Startup(object sender, StartupEventArgs e)
{
    new Bootstrapper().Run();
}
```

The last thing that needs to be done is to assign the MainPage to the RootVisual property of the App class. This is also done in the bootstrapper class, in the InitializeShell method override. The code in listing 1.3 shows the implementation.

Listing 1.3 – *Initializing the application's shell*
```
protected override void InitializeShell()
{
    var view = Shell as MainPage;
    App.Current.RootVisual = view;
}
```

The Bootstrapper.Shell property represents the value that was returned from the CreateShell method. In the InitializeShell method we can also assign a view-model to the view's DataContext property. Another initialization option might be to navigate to the initial view inside the main application region. The code in listing 1.4 presents this alternative.

Listing 1.4 – *Navigating to a view inside a region in order to display the initial UI*
```
protected override void InitializeShell()
{
    var view = Shell as MainPage;
    var vm = Container.Resolve<MainViewModel>();
    view.DataContext=vm;
    App.Current.RootVisual = view;
    IRegionManager rm = Container.Resolve<IRegionManager>();
    rm.RequestNavigate("MainRegion", "HomeView");
}
```

You can see that, in listing 1.4, we resolved the view-model using the Unity container. This ensures that any potential dependencies are also created and injected. After showing the Shell UI we navigate to the main view using the region manager. We'll talk in detail about regions and region navigation in later chapters, but the main thing to notice here is that we can override the InitializeShell method if we want to do further view initialization.

For a WPF application, the Run method can be called in the OnStartup method override of the App class. When overriding this method, make sure to remove the StartupUri attribute from the App.xaml file. The code in listing 1.5 shows how to initialize a WPF application.

Listing 1.5 – *Initializing a WPF application*
```
protected override void OnStartup(StartupEventArgs e)
{
    base.OnStartup(e);
    new Bootstrapper().Run();
}
```

The WPF InitializeShell implementation can be seen in listing 1.6. Make sure that you do not call ShowDialog when displaying the Shell view. This will prevent the application modules from being loaded.

Listing 1.6 – *Initializing the shell for a WPF application*
```
protected override void InitializeShell()
{
    var view = Shell as MainWindow;
    App.Current.MainWindow = view;
    App.Current.MainWindow.Show();
}
```

PRISM applications can also use MEF in order to resolve their dependencies. There is a lot of confusion about whether or not MEF is a DI container. The short answer is that it isn't. MEF was built with the purpose of providing a common framework for enabling add-in functionality for standard applications. Although being a dedicated DI container was not the first priority when MEF was conceived, it turns out that you can use it as one. If you are already familiar with MEF, you may choose to initialize your application by deriving from the MefBootstrapper class. The code in listing 1.7 shows such a bootstrapper implementation.

Listing 1.7 – *Deriving from MefBootstrapper*
```
public class Bootstrapper:MefBootstrapper
{
    protected override void ConfigureAggregateCatalog()
    {
        base.ConfigureAggregateCatalog();
        AggregateCatalog.Catalogs.Add(
          new AssemblyCatalog(this.GetType().Assembly));
    }
    protected override DependencyObject CreateShell()
    {
        return Container.GetExportedValue<MainWindow>();
    }
    protected override void InitializeShell()
    {
        App.Current.MainWindow = (MainWindow)Shell;
        App.Current.MainWindow.Show();
    }
}
```

There are two things that are worth mentioning in listing 1.7. The first is that we use the GetExportedValue method in order to obtain a Shell instance. Calling this method, instead of using the new keyword, assures us that any dependencies will also be satisfied. To use this method we need to add the Export attribute to the MainWindow class definition. The second thing to mention is that, in order for this to work, we need to register our exports/imports with the container. We do this by providing an AssemblyCatalog instance pointing to the current assembly. This assembly catalog is added to the collection of catalogs managed by the bootstrapper's aggregate catalog.

1.2 Bootstrapper features

The bootstrapper class is used to configure a number of application features. These features include: the logging service, the DI container, the module catalog, the service locator, the region manager and associated services and the Shell. All these steps need to happen in a particular order and this order is established in the Bootstrapper.Run method. Depending on the bootstrapper, the number of steps in the Run method might differ, but in general it should be the same regardless of the DI container that is used. Figure 1.1 presents these steps.

The default CreateLogger method returns a PRISM implementation of the ILoggerFacade interface. For WPF applications this is a TextLogger. For Silverlight an EmptyLogger is returned. If you want to change the logger that is used, all you have to do is to override the CreateLogger method. The code presented in listing 1.8 shows an example.

Listing 1.8 – *Changing the default logger*
```
protected override ILoggerFacade CreateLogger()
{
```

```
        return new TraceLogger();
}
```

When building modular applications it is important to specify how the modules are discovered and also the modules you want to use. These things can be done by overriding the bootstrapper's CreateModuleCatalog and ConfigureModuleCatalog methods. A ModuleCatalog instance represents a collection of ModuleInfo items. A ModuleInfo instance contains the metadata about a module: the module name, initialization mode and location.

If the ModuleCatalog instance, provided by default, does not suit your needs you can override the CreateModuleCatalog method in order to specify your own catalog. This can be seen in listing 1.9.

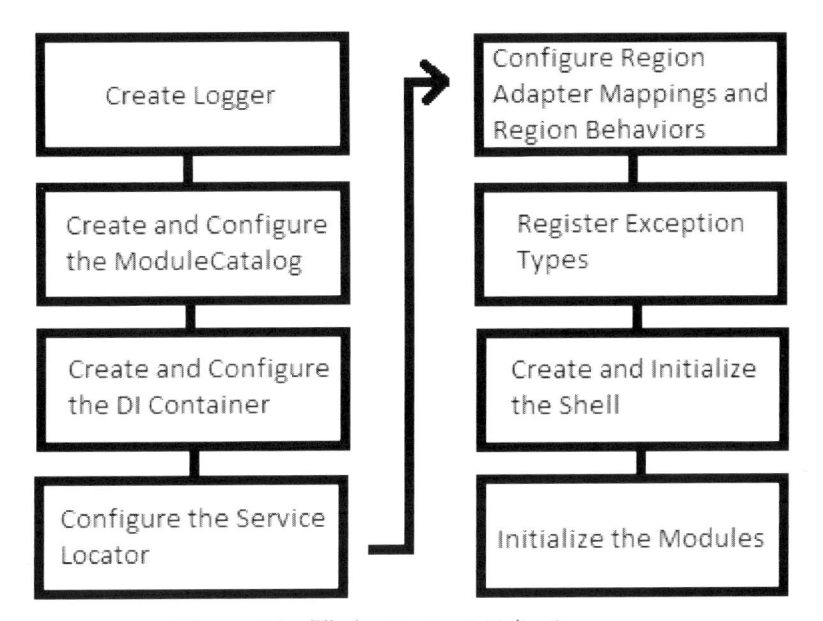

Figure 1.1 – *The bootstrapper initialization sequence*

Listing 1.9 – *Specifying a new module catalog*
```
protected override IModuleCatalog CreateModuleCatalog()
{
    return new DirectoryModuleCatalog() {
        ModulePath = @".\Modules" };
}
```

The implementation shown in listing 1.9 uses a DirectoryModuleCatalog instance in order to discover all modules at the specified directory location. The class will check all assemblies at the specified location for types that implement the IModule interface.

You can also add additional configuration to a module catalog by overriding the ConfigureModuleCatalog method. One such example is if you want to manually add other modules. These modules are almost always referenced by the Shell. The code shown in listing 1.10 presents an example. In this case, the Module1 module has been added to the list of modules that were retrieved by the DirectoryModuleCatalog instance.

Listing 1.10 – *Configuring the module catalog with additional modules*
```
protected override void ConfigureModuleCatalog()
{
    base.ConfigureModuleCatalog();
    Type mt = typeof(Module1);
    var mi = new ModuleInfo(mt.Name, mt.AssemblyQualifiedName);
    ModuleCatalog.AddModule(mi);
}
```

The DI container is usually created in the base bootstrapper class (UnityBootstrapper or MefBootstrapper) so there is usually no need to you to override the CreateContainer method. What you will have to override is the ConfigureContainer method in order to add new type registrations. These will allow the depending classes to be resolved properly. The way that types are registered will differ depending on the DI container you use. The UnityBootstrapper registers the core services like below.

```
RegisterTypeIfMissing(typeof(IRegionManager),
        typeof(RegionManager), true);
RegisterTypeIfMissing(typeof(IEventAggregator),
    typeof(EventAggregator), true);
```

The RegisterTypeIfMissing method is a protected method that registers a type only if that type hasn't been registered before. This might actually be a good thing since Unity overwrites existing type registrations if you register the same type again. To register your own service with the UnityContainer you can use the code in listing 1.11.

Listing 1.11 – *Registering application specific services*
```
protected override void ConfigureContainer()
{
    base.ConfigureContainer();
    Container.RegisterInstance<IInteractionService>(
        new InteractionService());
}
```

The MefBootstrapper bootstrapper makes use of a few instances of types that need to be used by other classes as well. These types are: the logger instance, the module catalog instance and others. In order for these instances to be used by other types we need to register them with the CompositionContainer. This is done in the ConfigureContainer method as listing 1.12 shows. When using MEF, the recommended way of registering types is by using attributes. This isn't possible in this case because these instances are used before the CompositionContainer is created in the bootstrapper initialization sequence.

Listing 1.12 – *MefBootstrapper core services registration*
```
protected virtual void RegisterBootstrapperProvidedTypes()
{
```

```csharp
    this.Container.ComposeExportedValue<ILoggerFacade>(
        this.Logger);
    this.Container.ComposeExportedValue<IModuleCatalog>(
        this.ModuleCatalog);
    this.Container.ComposeExportedValue<IServiceLocator>(
        new MefServiceLocatorAdapter(this.Container));
    this.Container.ComposeExportedValue<AggregateCatalog>(
        this.AggregateCatalog);
}
protected virtual void ConfigureContainer()
{
    this.RegisterBootstrapperProvidedTypes();
}
```

The MefBootstrapper class also offers 2 additional methods that are used for creating and configuring the AggregateCatalog catalog used by MEF. These are CreateAggregateCatalog and ConfigureAggregateCatalog. This allows you to register new types with the container in an imperative way. The code shown in listing 1.13 presents an example.

Listing 1.13 – *Adding modules to the aggregate catalog*
```csharp
protected override void ConfigureAggregateCatalog()
{
    base.ConfigureAggregateCatalog();
    this.AggregateCatalog.Catalogs.Add(
        new AssemblyCatalog(typeof(ModuleC.ModuleC).Assembly));
}
```

After the modules are configured, the next step in the bootstrapper initialization sequence is to configure the default region adapter mappings and region behaviors. You can override these methods if you need to add your own region adapter or region behavior implementations.

After the Shell is created and initialized, the bootstrapper will use the IModuleManager service to load and initialize the modules. This step allows modules to do things like: register views with the Shell regions, register module specific services and subscribe to application events. This happens because the IModuleManager implementation calls the Initialize method of every module that was registered with the ModuleCatalog. Module dependencies will be injected automatically when the module instance is resolved with the service locator which, in turn, accesses the DI container.

1.3 Custom bootstrappers

If we need to use a different bootstrapper then the ones provided out of the box by PRISM we can do that as well. There are 2 classes that we need to implement: a custom service locator adapter and a custom bootstrapper. Since PRISM is container agnostic, it uses the service locator in order to resolve object instances. To allow PRISM to use our container we need to tell it how to map the service locator calls to our container calls. The classic solution to this problem is to implement an adapter class.

The example presented here will use the CastleWindows DI container. You can download the binaries from their site at http://www.castleproject.org/projects/windsor/. The code shown in listing 1.14 presents the adapter implementation. Before adding this class definition make sure you add references to the following Windsor assemblies: Castle.Core.dll and Castle.Windsor.dll.

Listing 1.14 – *Implementing the service locator adapter*
```
public class WindsorContainerAdapter:ServiceLocatorImplBase
{
    Castle.Windsor.IWindsorContainer container;
    public WindsorContainerAdapter(
        Castle.Windsor.IWindsorContainer container)
    {
        this.container = container;
    }
    protected override IEnumerable<object> DoGetAllInstances(
        Type serviceType)
    {
        return (IEnumerable<object>)container.ResolveAll(
        serviceType);
    }
    protected override object DoGetInstance(Type serviceType,
        string key)
    {
        if (key == null)
            return container.Resolve(serviceType);
        else
            return container.Resolve(key, serviceType);
    }
}
```

In order to implement the bootstrapper we will use the UnityBootstrapper as an example. The first thing we need to do is to derive our custom class from the Bootstrapper base class. The code shown in listing 1.15 presents this implementation.

Listing 1.15 – *Deriving from the base Bootstrapper class*
```
public abstract class WindsorBootstrapper:Microsoft.Practices.Prism.Bootstrapper
{
    protected override void ConfigureServiceLocator()
    {
        throw new NotImplementedException();
    }
    public override void Run(bool runWithDefaultConfiguration)
    {
        throw new NotImplementedException();
    }
}
```

The base Bootstrapper class has three abstract methods. We will override only two of them. The third method, CreateShell, will be overridden in a derived class. Add the implementation for the ConfigureServiceLocator method as shown in listing 1.16.

Listing 1.16 – *Configuring the service locator*
```
protected override void ConfigureServiceLocator()
```

```
{
    ServiceLocator.SetLocatorProvider(() =>
        this.Container.Resolve<IServiceLocator>());
}
```

This method is used to configure the service locator provider. This provider will abstract the actual DI container that is used in order to provide a consistent interface for resolving types inside the PRISM framework. You can see that we use our specific DI container to resolve the locator provider as an instance of IServiceLocator. For this to work we need to register the IServiceLocator service with the container. We also need to create a WindsorContainer instance and assign it to the Container property. This property can be used in derived classes to register additional services. Add the property and method definition presented in listing 1.17 to create and expose the DI container.

Listing 1.17 – *Creating the DI container used by the bootstrapper*
```
public IWindsorContainer Container { get; protected set; }
protected virtual IWindsorContainer CreateContainer()
{
    return new WindsorContainer();
}
```

The next thing we need to do is to override the Run abstract method. We will use the diagram presented earlier in order to configure all the required services in the correct order. When doing this we should also look at the UnityBootstrapper implementation as an example.

The log will be created first since we need to log everything that happens in the application. Add the code presented in listing 1.18 to the beginning of the Run method.

Listing 1.18 – *Creating the application logger*
```
useDefaultConfiguration = runWithDefaultConfiguration;
this.Logger = this.CreateLogger();
if (this.Logger == null)
    throw new InvalidOperationException("Null logger");
this.Logger.Log("Logger created.", Category.Debug, Priority.Low);
```

Add the code presented in listing 1.19 in order to create and configure the module catalog.

Listing 1.19 – *Creating and configuring the module catalog*
```
this.Logger.Log("Creating module catalog...",
        Category.Debug, Priority.Low);
this.ModuleCatalog = this.CreateModuleCatalog();
if (this.ModuleCatalog == null)
    throw new InvalidOperationException("Null module catalog");
this.Logger.Log("Configuring module catalog...",
        Category.Debug, Priority.Low);
this.ConfigureModuleCatalog();
```

Below the module catalog configuration, add the code shown in listing 1.20 in order to create and configure the DI container.

Listing 1.20 *– Creating and configuring the DI container*
```
this.Logger.Log("Creating DI container",
        Category.Debug, Priority.Low);
this.Container = this.CreateContainer();
if (this.Container == null)
    throw new InvalidOperationException("Null container");
this.Logger.Log("Configuring container",
        Category.Debug, Priority.Low);
this.ConfigureContainer();
```

Next, we configure the service locator, region adapter mappings, region behaviors and we register the framework exception types. This can be seen in listing 1.21.

Listing 1.21 *– Configuring region adapters and behaviors*
```
this.Logger.Log("Configure service locator...",
        Category.Debug, Priority.Low);
this.ConfigureServiceLocator();
this.Logger.Log("Configure region adapters...",
        Category.Debug, Priority.Low);
this.ConfigureRegionAdapterMappings();
this.Logger.Log("Configure region behaviors...",
        Category.Debug, Priority.Low);
this.ConfigureDefaultRegionBehaviors();
this.Logger.Log("Registering exception types...",
        Category.Debug, Priority.Low);
this.RegisterFrameworkExceptionTypes();
```

The Shell is created and configured next. If the Shell is not null, we set the global region manager and update the regions. At the end we call the InitializeShell method which should display the UI. Add the code presented in listing 1.22 to create and initialize the Shell.

Listing 1.22 *– Creating and initializing the Shell*
```
this.Logger.Log("Creating Shell...",
        Category.Debug, Priority.Low);
this.Shell = this.CreateShell();
if (this.Shell != null)
{
    this.Logger.Log("Setting region manager",
            Category.Debug, Priority.Low);
    RegionManager.SetRegionManager(this.Shell,
            this.Container.Resolve<IRegionManager>());
    this.Logger.Log("Updating regions",
            Category.Debug, Priority.Low);
    RegionManager.UpdateRegions();
    this.Logger.Log("Initialising Shell",
            Category.Debug, Priority.Low);
    this.InitializeShell();
}
```

The last step in the bootstrapping process is to initialize the modules. This will allow each module to register its views and services with the application. Add the code presented in listing 1.23 in order to initialize the modules.

Listing 1.23 – *Initializing the application modules*
```
try
{
    var mm = Container.Resolve<IModuleManager>();
    this.Logger.Log("Initialising modules...",
        Category.Debug, Priority.Low);
    this.InitializeModules();
}
catch (Exception) { }
this.Logger.Log("Bootstrapper sequence completed",
    Category.Debug, Priority.Low);
```

Now that the bootstrapping process is complete we need to configure the core PRISM services. We'll do this in the ConfigureContainer method. Add the method definition presented in listing 1.24 to the WindsorBootstrapper class.

Listing 1.24 – *Configuring the core PRISM services*
```
protected virtual void ConfigureContainer()
{
    Container.Register(Component.For<IWindsorContainer>()
        .UsingFactoryMethod(() => { return Container; })
        .LifeStyle.Singleton);
    Container.Register(Component.For<ILoggerFacade>()
        .UsingFactoryMethod(() => { return Logger; })
        .LifeStyle.Singleton);
    Container.Register(Component.For<IModuleCatalog>()
        .UsingFactoryMethod(() => { return ModuleCatalog; })
        .LifeStyle.Singleton);
    Container.Register(Component.For<IServiceLocator>()
        .ImplementedBy<WindsorContainerAdapter>()
        .LifeStyle.Singleton);
}
```

At the beginning we register the container, logger, module catalog and service locator adapter. We register these services as singletons. We only need one instance of these services. After this we need to register the core services that handle event aggregation, regions and region navigation as well as module management. Add the code shown in listing 1.25 at the end of the ConfigureContainer method. Note that the list of registrations was taken from the UnityBootstrapper implementation and was adapted for the Windsor container.

Listing 1.25 – *Registering the core PRISM services*
```
Container.Register(Component.For<IModuleInitializer>()
    .ImplementedBy<ModuleInitializer>().LifeStyle.Singleton);
Container.Register(Component.For<IModuleManager>()
    .ImplementedBy<ModuleManager>().LifeStyle.Singleton);
Container.Register(Component.For<RegionAdapterMappings>()
```

```
        .ImplementedBy<RegionAdapterMappings>().LifeStyle.Singleton);
Container.Register(Component.For<IRegionManager>()
        .ImplementedBy<RegionManager>().LifeStyle.Singleton);
Container.Register(Component.For<IEventAggregator>()
        .ImplementedBy<EventAggregator>().LifeStyle.Singleton);
Container.Register(Component.For<IRegionViewRegistry>()
        .ImplementedBy<RegionViewRegistry>().LifeStyle.Singleton);
Container.Register(Component.For<IRegionBehaviorFactory>()
        .ImplementedBy<RegionBehaviorFactory>().LifeStyle.Singleton);
Container.Register(Component.For<IRegionNavigationJournalEntry>()
        .ImplementedBy<RegionNavigationJournalEntry>()
            .LifeStyle.Transient);
Container.Register(Component.For<IRegionNavigationJournal>()
        .ImplementedBy<RegionNavigationJournal>()
            .LifeStyle.Transient);
Container.Register(Component.For<IRegionNavigationService>()
        .ImplementedBy<RegionNavigationService>()
            .LifeStyle.Transient);
Container.Register(Component
            .For<IRegionNavigationContentLoader>()
        .ImplementedBy<RegionNavigationContentLoader>()
        .LifeStyle.Singleton);
```

Notice that the region navigation service, journal and journal entry services are registered as transient services. This is required because each region should have its own navigation service and journal. Also we need new journal entries every time we navigate inside the region. We will talk about these services in detail in later chapters so there is no need to worry if you don't know what they do at this time.

CastleWindsor is different from UnityContainer when it comes to resolving types. In order to resolve any type with CastleWindsor we first need to register it. This is also true when it comes to registering concrete classes. Unity can resolve concrete classes even if they were not previously registered. This poses a problem when using Windsor because PRISM resolves some region specific concrete classes that were not previously registered. Specifically, it resolves the region adapters and region behaviors. The last lines of code we need to add to the ConfigureContainer method refer to registering the region adapters and region behaviors.

Most of the region functionality is not contained in IRegion implementations, but in region behaviors. View discovery, for example, is implemented as a region behavior and so is a view's lifetime inside a region as well as many other features. PRISM knows what behaviors to apply to a particular region by using a region behavior factory. This factory provides default behaviors that are applied to all regions in the application. The behaviors are held inside a dictionary and the keys can be iterated over.

The method that adds region behaviors to this region behavior factory is called ConfigureDefaultRegionBehaviors and is defined in the base Bootstrapper class. This method is then invoked from the Run method of our derived bootstrapper class. PRISM applies the region behaviors in the region adapters by iterating over the keys contained in the region behavior factory and instantiating new behavior instances. At this point the region behavior types need to be registered with Windsor, otherwise we'll get an error.

Since the container is configured before the region adapters apply the region behaviors we could register our behavior and adapter types in the ConfigureContainer method override. Another option is to add some logic to the service locator adapter implementation. Add the helper methods presented in listing 1.26 to the WindsorContainerAdapter class definition.

Listing 1.26 – *Helper methods to determine if we should register a particular service type*
```
private bool IsRegionBehavior(Type serviceType)
{
    bool res = serviceType ==
        typeof(DelayedRegionCreationBehavior) ||
        (!serviceType.IsInterface && !serviceType.IsAbstract &&
        typeof(IRegionBehavior).IsAssignableFrom(serviceType));
    return res;
}
private bool IsRegionAdapter(Type serviceType)
{
    return typeof(IRegionAdapter)
        .IsAssignableFrom(serviceType) &&
        !serviceType.IsInterface && !serviceType.IsAbstract;
}
```

The methods in listing 1.26 help us determine if a service type is a region adapter or a region behavior. We use these methods in the adapter's GetInstance implementation to determine if we should register the types before trying to resolve them again. Modify the GetInstance implementation as shown in listing 1.27.

Listing 1.27 – *Resolving types from WindsorContainerAdapter*
```
protected override object DoGetInstance(Type serviceType,
        string key)
{
    try
    {
        if (key == null)
            return container.Resolve(serviceType);
        else
            return container.Resolve(key, serviceType);
    }
    catch (ComponentNotFoundException)
    {
        if (IsRegionBehavior(serviceType) ||
         IsRegionAdapter(serviceType))
        {
            container.Register(Component.For(serviceType)
                .LifeStyle.Transient);
            return container.Resolve(serviceType);
        }
        throw;
    }
}
```

We added a try-catch block to the implementation. If we cannot resolve a particular type we enter the catch clause where we check the type that could not be resolved. If that type is a region adapter or a region behavior, we register it with the Windsor container and we resolve it again. This has the effect of resolving the concrete classes even if they were not explicitly registered before.

In order to use this bootstrapper we need to derive from it and override the CreateShell method, just like with the implementations offered by PRISM. We can also register our application specific services by overriding the ConfigureContainer method.

1.4 Custom logging

Logging in PRISM can be done by using the ILoggerFacade service. The service has a single method named Log. The interface definition can be seen in listing 1.28.

Listing 1.28 – *The logging service interface*
```
public interface ILoggerFacade
{
    void Log(string message, Category category,
        Priority priority);
}
```

The message category is identified by the Category enumeration. We can have the following categories: Debug, Exception, Information and Warning.

The message priority is identified by the Priority enumeration. We can have the following message priorities: None, High, Medium and Low.

Prism offers 3 out of the box implementations of the ILoggerFacade service: EmptyLogger, TextLogger and TraceLogger. The EmptyLogger implementation does nothing. It is the default logger used for Silverlight applications. The TextLogger implementation writes the text messages to a TextWriter. The default constructor writes messages to the output window. This is the default logger used for WPF applications. The TraceLogger implementation writes the text messages to the Trace class. This implementation is only available in WPF.

The logger for a composite application is created in the bootstrapper's CreateLogger method. The code in listing 1.29 shows the override for a WPF application. This logger writes text messages to the specified file.

Listing 1.29 – *Supplying a new logger that writes to a specified file*
```
protected override ILoggerFacade CreateLogger()
{
    var writer = new StreamWriter("d:\\log.txt");
    return new TextLogger(writer);
}
```

We could also implement this service to use the very popular log4net logging framework. This can be done by implementing an adapter class and will allow us to use a lot of the features offered by log4net including: xml configuration, database logging and more. The code in listing 1.30 presents such an adapter.

Listing 1.30 – *Creating a custom logger*
```
public class CustomLogger:ILoggerFacade
```

```csharp
{
    private ILog log;
    public CustomLogger()
    {
        log4net.Config.XmlConfigurator.Configure();
        log = log4net.LogManager.GetCurrentLoggers()
            .Where(p => p.Logger.Name == "MainLog")
          .FirstOrDefault();
    }
    public void Log(string message, Category category,
        Priority priority)
    {
        switch(category)
        {
            case Category.Debug:
                log.Debug(message);
                break;
            case Category.Exception:
                log.Error(message);
                break;
            case Category.Info:
                log.Info(message);
                break;
            case Category.Warn:
                log.Warn(message);
                break;
        }
    }
}
```

The configuration for the MainLog logger can be seen in listing 1.31.

Listing 1.31 – *Configuring the log4net logger*
```xml
<configSections>
  <section name="log4net" type="log4net.Config.Log4NetConfigurationSectionHandler, log4net"/>
</configSections>
<log4net>
  <appender name="TextFileAppender" type="log4net.Appender.RollingFileAppender">
    <file value="D:\AppLog.txt"/>
    <appendToFile value="true"/>
    <rollingStyle value="Size"/>
    <maxSizeRollBackups value="10"/>
    <maximumFileSize value="10000KB"/>
    <staticLogFileName value="true"/>
    <layout type="log4net.Layout.PatternLayout">
      <conversionPattern value="%date{dd.MM.yyyy HH:mm:ss} [%identity] %-5level %class.%method: %message%newline"/>
    </layout>
  </appender>
  <logger name="MainLog">
    <level value="DEBUG"/>
```

```xml
    <appender-ref ref="TextFileAppender"/>
  </logger>
</log4net>
```

This custom logger can now be used in the CreateLogger bootstrapper override.

1.5 Summary

This chapter talked about initializing PRISM applications. Implementing a composite application can be difficult at first. A few things need to be configured before showing the UI and you need to commit to using some best practices in order to successfully develop the application in such a way that makes it easy to test, maintain and extend.

Any PRISM application needs to run some initialization logic before showing the UI. This is because multiple PRISM services need to be set up for everything to work correctly. All this initialization code is contained in a central place called the bootstrapper. PRISM provides two bootstrappers out of the box: UnityBootstrapper and MefBootstrapper. These bootstrappers use the UnityContainer and MEF respectively in order to satisfy object dependencies.

The bootstrapper offers a lot of extensibility points. We can configure the DI container, the module catalog, the application services and the logger among others.

CHAPTER 2: MODULAR APPLICATIONS

A modular application is an application composed of several functional units. These units are the modules and they contain separate pieces of application functionality. The modules are loaded into the application in order to provide the entire application functionality.

Modules are independent of each other but they can still communicate with one another in a loosely coupled way. Modules can contain pieces of the UI or BL. Modules can also contain application level services such as logging and authentication.

By using modules your application will be easier to develop, test, maintain and extend. The application modules can also be developed in parallel, leading to faster development if multiple developers are involved.

2.1 Modules

A module is a logical collection of functionality that can be packaged in one or more assemblies or in a XAP file. All modules have a central class that is used to integrate the module functionality into the application. This central class is defined by implementing the IModule interface. This interface exposes a single method, Initialize, which is used to initialize the module. In this method, the module can register its services and views with the application. Here the module can also subscribe to application events or services. Listing 2.1 presents a possible module definition.

Listing 2.1 – *Implementing the IModule interface*
```
public class Module2 : IModule
{
    private IRegionManager regMgr;
    public Module2(IRegionManager regMgr)
    {
        this.regMgr = regMgr;
    }
    public void Initialize()
    {
        regMgr.RegisterViewWithRegion("DemoRegion",
          () => { return "hello from module2."; });
    }
```

}

In this example, the module registers its view with the application region manager. When the time comes to display the specified region, the region will load the specified view. Module instances are resolved using a DI container. This allows module dependencies to be injected into the constructor (the IRegionManager service) before the module is properly initialized. We can have multiple modules defined in the same assembly or we can have a single module definition per assembly. This all depends on your requirements. All modules that need to be used by an application must be defined in a module catalog.

2.2 Module Catalogs

A module catalog is an implementation of the IModuleCatalog service. PRISM provides several implementations of this interface in order to load modules from memory or from a particular location on disk for module assemblies that are not directly referenced by the Shell assembly. Modules not directly referenced by the Shell assembly can be configured using: a configuration file, a XAML file or a disk location.

The ModuleCatalog class is the default catalog implementation used by PRISM with the UnityBootstrapper bootstrapper. The type can be used to load modules that have their assemblies already referenced by the Shell. This can be done by using the AddModule method. Listing 2.2 presents an example that adds a module to the catalog in the ConfigureModuleCatalog method of the bootstrapper.

Listing 2.2 – *Adding a module to the module catalog by using code*
```
protected override void ConfigureModuleCatalog()
{
    Type mt = typeof(Module1.Module1);
    var mi = new ModuleInfo(mt.Name, mt.AssemblyQualifiedName);
    ModuleCatalog.AddModule(mi);
}
```

The MethodInfo type contains all the metadata about a particular module. This includes: the module name, the module type, the list of modules this module depends on, the initialization mode and the location of the module assembly. The initialization mode specifies whether the module is to be loaded when the application starts or explicitly by the user. The initialization mode is specified by using the InitializationMode enumeration. This enumeration can be seen below.

```
public enum InitializationMode { WhenAvailable, OnDemand }
```

The ModuleCatalog type can also be used to load module assemblies from a XAML file. This option allows the loading of modules without having a direct reference to the modules' assemblies from the Shell assembly. In order to load the modules this way we need to use the CreateFromXaml static method. Listing 2.3 presents such an example. Here, the CreateModuleCatalog method is overridden in the bootstrapper in order to create the catalog.

Listing 2.3 – *Creating a module catalog from a XAML file*
```
protected override IModuleCatalog CreateModuleCatalog()
```

```
{
    return Microsoft.Practices.Prism.Modularity
        ModuleCatalog.CreateFromXaml( new Uri(
        "/ModuleUnity1;component/modules.xaml",
        UriKind.Relative));
}
```

The XAML file is included in the Shell assembly named ModuleUnity1 as a resource. The XAML file is called modules.xaml. Listing 2.4 presents the structure of such a XAML file.

Listing 2.4 – *Defining a module catalog in XAML*
```
<m:ModuleCatalog xmlns="http://schemas.microsoft.com/winfx/2006/xaml/presentation"
xmlns:x="http://schemas.microsoft.com/winfx/2006/xaml" xmlns:m="clr-
namespace:Microsoft.Practices.Prism.Modularity;assembly=Microsoft.Practices.Prism"
xmlns:sys="clr-namespace:System;assembly=mscorlib">
    <m:ModuleInfo ModuleName="Module2"
        Ref="file://Modules/Module2.dll"
        ModuleType="Module2.Module2, Module2"/>
    <m:ModuleInfo ModuleName="Module3"
        Ref="file://Modules/Module3.dll"
        ModuleType="Module3.Module3, Module3, Version=1.0.0.0, Culture=neutral, Public
KeyToken=null"/>
</m:ModuleCatalog>
```

This XAML file specifies 2 modules located in the Modules folder under the executable path. Using a XAML file also gives us the option of grouping multiple modules. This is useful if we have multiple modules with the same location or initialization mode. Listing 2.5 presents such a module group.

Listing 2.5 – *Defining a module group*
```
<m:ModuleInfoGroup InitializationMode="WhenAvailable"
        Ref="file://Modules/Modules.dll">
    <m:ModuleInfo ModuleName="Module2"
            ModuleType="Module2.Module2, Module2"/>
    <m:ModuleInfo ModuleName="Module3"
            ModuleType="Module3.Module3, Module3"/>
</m:ModuleInfoGroup>
```

In the XAML code from listing 2.5, the 2 modules are located in the same assembly and they both need to be loaded at application startup. Before adding a module to a module group, the module properties are overwritten if they have default values. This means a module can decide its location and initialization mode even if it's contained in a group.

The CreateFromXaml static method has an overload that accepts a Stream. This version can be used when the XAML file that defines the module catalog is supplied as a content file, separate from the Shell assembly. This allows us to modify the module catalog content without recompiling the application. Listing 2.6 shows how to create a ModuleCatalog instance from such a file.

Listing 2.6 – *Creating a module catalog from a stream*
```
protected override IModuleCatalog CreateModuleCatalog()
```

```
{
    using (var stream = new FileStream("content_modules.xaml",
        FileMode.Open, FileAccess.Read))
    {
        return Microsoft.Practices.Prism.Modularity
            .ModuleCatalog.CreateFromXaml(stream);
    }
}
```

The XAML configuration works great when the module location is either absolute or the module is in the current executable path. Trying to specify a relative directory location under the executable path won't work. In order to fix this we need to make some changes to the default FileModuleTypeLoader implementation. The details will be presented when we talk about custom module type loaders later in the chapter.

Another issue that arises in some cases when using a XAML file to define the module catalog is that a XamlParseException exception is thrown saying that an invalid character was found, even if the file is syntactically correct. One such exception can be seen below. A simple solution to this problem is to copy the contents into a simple text file.

", hexadecimal value 0x0C, is an invalid character. Line 1, position 1.

The ConfigurationModuleCatalog class can be used to load modules from the application configuration file. The module assemblies don't need to be referenced by the Shell assembly. The catalog can be created in the bootstrapper's CreateModuleCatalog method. Listing 2.7 presents the code.

Listing 2.7 – *Creating a configuration module catalog*
```
protected override IModuleCatalog CreateModuleCatalog()
{
    return new ConfigurationModuleCatalog();
}
```

The structure of the configuration file is presented in listing 2.8.

Listing 2.8 – *Defining the module catalog in the configuration*
```
<configuration>
  <configSections>
    <section name="modules" type="Microsoft.Practices.Prism.Modularity.ModulesConfigura
tionSection, Microsoft.Practices.Prism"/>
  </configSections>
  <modules>
    <module assemblyFile="Modules\Module2.dll"
            moduleType="Module2.Module2, Module2"
            moduleName="Module2" startupLoaded="False" >
    </module>
  </modules>
</configuration>
```

The configuration file first defines the necessary configuration section. After this, the modules are defined. The above configuration file contains a single module named Module2 that is located in the Modules folder under the executable path. The module path could have also been specified like this: '.\Modules\Module2.dll'. The module is to be loaded explicitly by the user. The startupLoaded property is used to set the InitializationMode value on the ModuleInfo instance.

In order to load module assemblies by doing a directory sweep we need to use the DirectoryModuleCatalog class. This class specifies a ModulePath property that can be used to specify the directory location where the module assemblies are located. Listing 2.9 presents the bootstrapper method where the catalog is created. A relative path is specified in this listing.

Listing 2.9 – *Creating a module catalog using a directory sweep*
```
protected override IModuleCatalog CreateModuleCatalog()
{
    return new DirectoryModuleCatalog() {
        ModulePath = @".\Modules" };
}
```

In listing 2.9, the module path could have been specified also like this: 'Modules'. The DirectoryModuleCatalog and ConfigurationModuleCatalog classes can be used only in WPF.

2.3 Module dependencies and initialization modes

Modules can depend on one another. Modules can depend only on modules defined in the same module group. A module's dependencies are defined in the DependsOn property. This property is a collection of strings that represents the module names of the modules the current module depends on. Module dependencies can also be specified in the following ways: in the XAML file, in the configuration file or by using attributes when defining the module classes. Listing 2.10 presents the code used to register a module with 2 dependencies.

Listing 2.10 – *Adding module dependencies in code*
```
protected override void ConfigureModuleCatalog()
{
    Type mt = typeof(Module1.Module1);
    var mi = new ModuleInfo(mt.Name, mt.AssemblyQualifiedName);
    mi.DependsOn = new Collection<string>() {
        "Module2", "Module3"
    };
    ModuleCatalog.AddModule(mi);
}
```

The same thing can be done in the XAML catalog as shown in listing 2.11.

Listing 2.11 – *Configuring dependencies between modules in XAML*
```
<m:ModuleCatalog xmlns="http://schemas.microsoft.com/winfx/2006/xaml/presentation"
xmlns:x="http://schemas.microsoft.com/winfx/2006/xaml" xmlns:m="clr-
namespace:Microsoft.Practices.Prism.Modularity;assembly=Microsoft.Practices.Prism"
xmlns:sys="clr-namespace:System;assembly=mscorlib">
    <m:ModuleInfo ModuleName="Module2"
        Ref="file://Modules/Module2.dll"
```

```xml
            ModuleType="Module2.Module2, Module2"/>
        <m:ModuleInfo ModuleName="Module3"
            Ref="file://Modules/Module3.dll"
            ModuleType="Module3.Module3, Module3"/>
        <m:ModuleInfo ModuleName="Module1"
            Ref="file://Modules/Module1.dll"
            ModuleType="Module1.Module1, Module1">
            <m:ModuleInfo.DependsOn>
                <sys:String>Module2</sys:String>
                <sys:String>Module3</sys:String>
            </m:ModuleInfo.DependsOn>
        </m:ModuleInfo>
</m:ModuleCatalog>
```

The same thing can be done in the configuration file as can be seen in listing 2.12.

Listing 2.12 – *Specifying module dependencies in the configuration file*
```xml
<modules>
    <module assemblyFile="Modules\Module1.dll"
            moduleType="Module1.Module1, Module1"
            moduleName="Module1" startupLoaded="true" >
        <dependencies>
            <dependency moduleName="Module2"/>
            <dependency moduleName="Module3"/>
        </dependencies>
    </module>
</modules>
```

Specifying module dependencies declaratively, by using the ModuleDependencyAttribute attribute, is useful when loading modules via directory sweep. This is because, in this case, the other options are not available. Listing 2.13 shows how to use this attribute.

Lisitng 2.13 – *Specifying module dependencies by using attributes*
```csharp
[ModuleDependency("Module2")]
[ModuleDependency("Module3")]
public class Module1 : IModule
{
    private IRegionManager regionManager;
    public Module1(IRegionManager regionManager)
    {
        this.regionManager = regionManager;
    }
    public void Initialize()
    {
        Debug.WriteLine("Module1 was initialized.");
    }
}
```

The ModuleDependencyAttribute attribute accepts only a single constructor argument. In order to specify multiple module dependencies, the attribute needs to be applied multiple times. The

ModuleAttribute attribute can be used when the name of the module is different from the name of the class that implements the IModule interface. Listing 2.14 presents how to use this attribute.

Listing 2.14 – *Setting the module name and initialization mode*
```
[Module(ModuleName = "MyModule", OnDemand = false)]
public class Module1 : IModule
{
    private IRegionManager regionManager;
    public Module1(IRegionManager regionManager)
    {
        this.regionManager = regionManager;
    }
    public void Initialize()
    {
        Debug.WriteLine("Module1 was initialized.");
    }
}
```

The OnDemand property in listing 2.14 specifies that the module is to be loaded at application startup. One thing that needs to be mentioned is that a module that is loaded at application startup cannot depend on a module that should be loaded on demand. OnDemand modules can only be loaded by explicitly calling the IModuleManager.LoadModule method.

2.4 Module Managers and Initializers

A module manager is used to coordinate all module loading features. These include: module assembly download, loading module assemblies into memory and instantiating and initializing modules.

IModuleManager is the service that handles the module management features. The only PRISM implementation is the ModuleManager class. This implementation uses an IModuleCatalog implementation to determine the modules to be managed and an IModuleInitializer implementation to instantiate and initialize the modules after their assemblies have been loaded into memory. Module loading can be done in two ways: on application startup or on demand. The modules that need to be loaded at application startup are loaded by calling the manager's Run method. Modules that need to be loaded on demand are loaded by using the manager's LoadModule method explicitly.

Module assembly loading is done by using an IModuleTypeLoader implementation. The last step in the bootstrapper initialization sequence is to load all modules that have an InitializationMode of WhenAvailable so the Run method does not need to be called explicitly. Listing 2.15 shows how to load a module explicitly.

Listing 2.15 – *Explicitly loading modules*
```
private void OnLoad()
{
    moduleManager.LoadModule("Module2");
}
```

Using the module manager we can monitor the module download progress. Listing 2.16 shows the code that subscribes to the appropriate events. The LoadModuleCompletedEventArgs class contains an IsErrorHandled property. This can be set to true if there is an error while loading the module and we don't want PRISM to throw an exception.

Listing 2.16 – *Monitoring module loading progress*
```
private IModuleManager moduleManager;
public MainViewModel(IModuleManager moduleManager)
{
    this.moduleManager = moduleManager;
    this.moduleManager.LoadModuleCompleted
        += LoadModuleCompleted;
}
void LoadModuleCompleted(object sender,
        LoadModuleCompletedEventArgs e)
{
    if (e.Error != null)
    {
        e.IsErrorHandled = true;
        return;
    }
    Debug.WriteLine(string.Format("Finished loading {0}",
        e.ModuleInfo.ModuleName));
}
```

A module initializer is used by the module manager in order to instantiate and initialize modules after their assemblies have been loaded. IModuleInitializer is the service that offers this functionality. The default implementation offered by PRISM is ModuleInitializer. The ModuleInitializer's job is to instantiate the module and to call its Initialize method. In order to instantiate a module, the initializer uses the IServiceLocator service to resolve the instance. The IServiceLocator implementation uses the DI container to resolve the module dependencies before creating and returning the module instance. After instantiation the Initialize method is called on the module in order to register its services with the application.

2.5 Building a modular application
In order to show how to build modular applications we will create a modular Silverlight application. The application is composed of 2 modules. One module will be loaded at application startup and the other will be loaded on demand when the user presses a button. The application will monitor the module download progress and will use Unity as the DI container.

Creating the Silverlight projects
To start this application, we create a new Silverlight application and host it in a web site. There is no need to enable RIA services. This will be the application Shell into which we will load our modules. We will add another 2 Silverlight application projects to the existing solution. These will be our 2 modules. We'll name the first project ModuleA. When creating this project we will host it in the same site as the Shell and we will uncheck the 'Add a test page that references the application' option because we don't want to access this functionality directly. This can be seen in figure 2.1.

Figure 2.1 – *Creating the Silverlight shell project*

Since we will use this project only to package the module functionality we don't need to keep the App.xaml and MainPage.xaml files. Delete these 2 files next. The second project, representing the ModuleB module, will be added in the same way. At the end, the project structure will look like the one presented in figure 2.2.

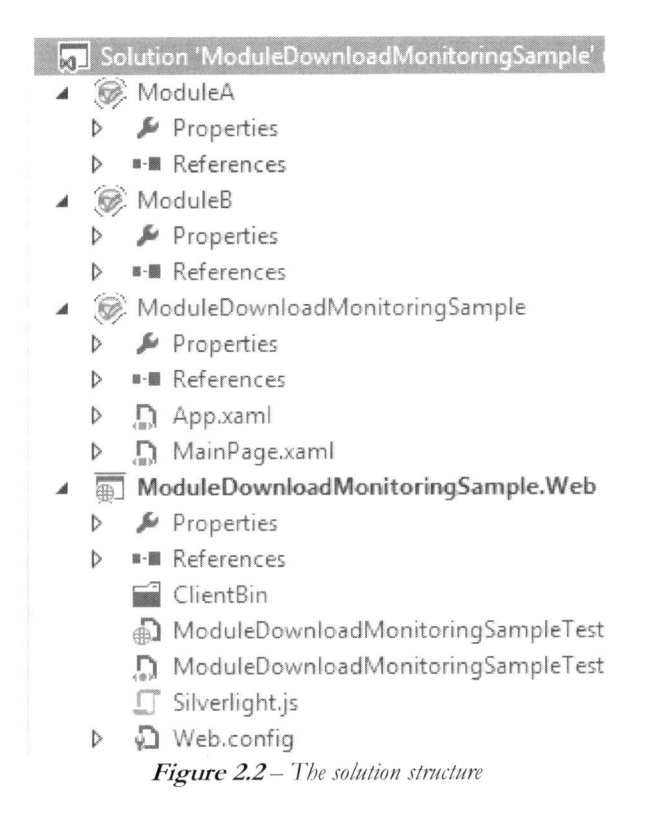

Figure 2.2 – *The solution structure*

Now that we have the projects set up, we should add the references to the PRISM library assemblies. We need to add references to all three projects. We need to add the following references to the Shell project: Microsoft.Practices.Prism.dll, Microsoft.Practices.Prism.UnityExtensions.dll and Microsoft.Practices.Unity.Silverlight.dll. These assemblies contain the modularity functionality as well as the Unity container and bootstrapper. For the other two Silverlight projects, that represent the modules, we need to add references to the following assemblies: Microsoft.Practices.Prism.dll and Microsoft.Practices.Unity.Silverlight.dll.

Initializing the application

Now that we have all the references set up, it's time to initialize our application. We need to create a new bootstrapper class in the Shell project. The code for this class can be seen in listing 2.17.

Listing 2.17 – *The bootstrapper definition*
```
public class Bootstrapper:UnityBootstrapper
{
    protected override DependencyObject CreateShell()
    {
        return new MainPage();
    }
    protected override void InitializeShell()
    {
        base.InitializeShell();
        var shell = (MainPage)Shell;
        shell.DataContext = Container.Resolve<MainViewModel>();
        App.Current.RootVisual = shell;
    }
}
```

The CreateShell method override will return our Shell UI and in the InitializeShell override we set up the Shell's DataContext property by resolving an instance of the MainViewModel class. This sample will be built using the MVVM approach. The MainViewModel class will represent our single view-model and it will contain all the application functionality. Resolving it from the container will allow all dependencies to be injected correctly.

In order to finish the application initialization we need to use our bootstrapper to display the Shell UI. For this we need to run the bootstrapper in the Application_Startup event handler. Listing 2.18 presents this handler.

Listing 2.18 – *Initializing the application*
```
private void Application_Startup(object sender,
        StartupEventArgs e)
{
    Bootstrapper b = new Bootstrapper();
    b.Run();
}
```

Monitoring the module download progress

The MainViewModel view-model class has a single dependency on the module manager service. We will use this service to monitor the module download progress. The code for the view-model class should look like the one presented in listing 2.19.

Listing 2.19 – *The application view-model definition*
```csharp
public class MainViewModel
{
    private IModuleManager moduleManager;
    public MainViewModel(IModuleManager moduleManager)
    {
        this.moduleManager = moduleManager;
        this.moduleManager.ModuleDownloadProgressChanged
          += ProgressChanged;
        this.moduleManager.LoadModuleCompleted
          += LoadModuleCompleted;
    }

    void LoadModuleCompleted(object sender,
         LoadModuleCompletedEventArgs e)
    {
        if (e.Error != null)
        {
            e.IsErrorHandled = true;
            var msg = string.Format("Error loading {0}",
                e.ModuleInfo.ModuleName);
            Debug.WriteLine(msg);
            return;
        }
        Debug.WriteLine(string.Format("Finished loading {0}",
          e.ModuleInfo.ModuleName));
    }

    void ProgressChanged(object sender,
         ModuleDownloadProgressChangedEventArgs e)
    {
        Debug.WriteLine(string.Format("{0} - {1}",
          e.ModuleInfo.ModuleName, e.ProgressPercentage));
    }
    //...
}
```

The MainViewModel view-model class subscribes to the two IModuleManager events. The ModuleDownloadProgressChanged event indicates the module download progress. The handler for this event exposes a ModuleDownloadProgressChangedEventArgs instance that exposes the BytesReceived and TotalBytesToReceive properties. These properties represent the downloaded bytes and the total module bytes respectively. The instance also exposes a property that returns the download percentage and the ModuleInfo instance that represents the metadata for the module that is downloaded.

The LoadModuleCompleted event is raised when the module has finished downloading either successfully or with an error. The Error property of the LoadModuleCompletedEventArgs instance indicates the error if any. This instance also exposes the IsErrorHandled property. This property can be set to true if we don't want PRISM to log and throw an exception if the module download fails.

The only thing left to do in the view-model is to define the command that will explicitly load the second module. We can use the PRISM DelegateCommand for this. The command and its

CanExecute handler can be seen in listing 2.20. We will load an additional, nonexistent, module (ModuleC) in order to simulate a module download error.

Listing 2.20 – *The Load command definition*
```
private DelegateCommand loadCmd;
public DelegateCommand LoadCommand
{
    get
    {
        if (loadCmd == null)
            loadCmd = new DelegateCommand(OnLoad);
        return loadCmd;
    }
}
private void OnLoad()
{
    moduleManager.LoadModule("ModuleB");
    moduleManager.LoadModule("ModuleC");
}
```

Creating the module catalog

Silverlight applications can configure a module catalog either in memory or with a XAML file. We will define our module catalog in a XAML file named modules.xaml. The file will be created in the Shell project. The structure for this file can be seen in listing 2.21.

Listing 2.21 – *Defining the module catalog in a XAML file*
```
<m:ModuleCatalog
    xmlns="http://schemas.microsoft.com/winfx/2006/xaml/presentation" xmlns:x="http://schemas.microsoft.com/winfx/2006/xaml"
    xmlns:m="clr-
namespace:Microsoft.Practices.Prism.Modularity;assembly=Microsoft.Practices.Prism" >
    <m:ModuleInfo Ref="ModuleA.xap" ModuleName="ModuleA"
        ModuleType="ModuleA.ModuleA, ModuleA, Version=1.0.0.0"/>
    <m:ModuleInfo Ref="ModuleB.xap" ModuleName="ModuleB"
        ModuleType="ModuleB.ModuleB, ModuleB, Version=1.0.0.0"
        InitializationMode="OnDemand"/>
    <m:ModuleInfo Ref="ModuleC.xap" ModuleName="ModuleC"
        ModuleType="ModuleC.ModuleC, ModuleC, Version=1.0.0.0"
        InitializationMode="OnDemand"/>
</m:ModuleCatalog>
```

The ModuleA module will be loaded at application startup while the other two modules will be loaded on demand. The code in listing 2.22 presents the bootstrapper method override that creates the module catalog based on this XAML file.

Listing 2.22 – *Creating the module catalog from the XAML file*
```
protected override IModuleCatalog CreateModuleCatalog(){
    var mc = Microsoft.Practices.Prism.Modularity
        .ModuleCatalog.CreateFromXaml( new Uri(
        "/ModuleDownloadMonitoringSample;component/modules.xaml",
```

```
        UriKind.Relative));
        return mc;
}
```

Creating the Shell view and initializing the modules

The last thing we need to do in the Shell project is to create the UI. This is easily done. We only need to display a button that is linked to the view-model command and an ItemsControl that will display the content from the 2 modules. The UI code for the Shell is presented in listing 2.23.

Listing 2.23 – *The Shell view definition. The Shell view will present a list of items.*
```xml
<Grid x:Name="LayoutRoot" Background="White">
    <Grid.RowDefinitions>
        <RowDefinition Height="auto"/>
        <RowDefinition/>
    </Grid.RowDefinitions>
    <Button Content="Load" Command="{Binding LoadCommand}"/>
    <ItemsControl Grid.Row="1"
        prism:RegionManager.RegionName="DemoRegion">
    </ItemsControl>
</Grid>
```

The ItemsControl defines a region that will display UI elements. We will talk about regions in a later chapter. In this example we will use the modules to add strings to the DemoRegion region. The prism namespace prefix is defined below.

```
xmlns:prism="http://www.codeplex.com/prism"
```

The module initialization code will be almost the same for both modules with the exception that the modules will register different strings with the DemoRegion region. Listing 2.24 presents the ModuleA module definition. The ModuleB module is implemented in the same way. Also remember to include the two PRISM assemblies mentioned at the beginning of the example.

Listing 2.24 – *Defining the ModuleA module. ModuleB is defined in the same way.*
```csharp
public class ModuleA : IModule
{
    private IRegionManager regionManager;
    public ModuleA(IRegionManager regionManager)
    {
        this.regionManager = regionManager;
    }
    public void Initialize()
    {
        regionManager.RegisterViewWithRegion("DemoRegion",
            () => { return "Module A string."; });
    }
}
```

Running the application now will give us a user interface similar to the one presented in figure 2.3.

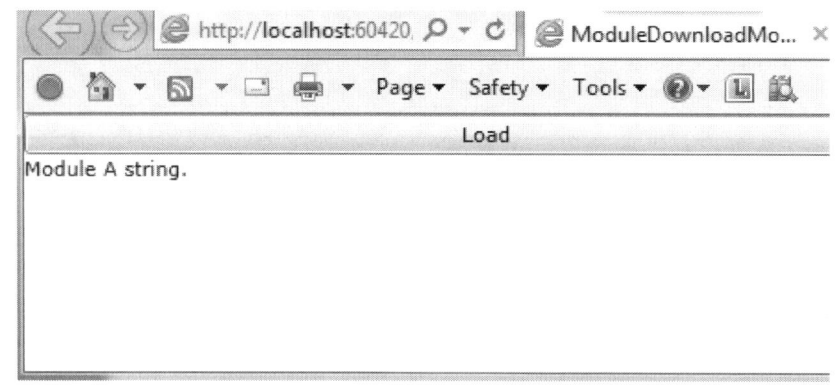

Figure 2.3 – *Running the modular application*

Pressing the load button should display the string for the ModuleB module as well and not throw an exception when the ModuleC module fails to load.

Writing modular applications for WPF is done the same way. The only difference is that we have more options regarding the module catalog configuration. We can configure the module catalog also by using a configuration file or directory sweep. All we need to do is write the code in the bootstrapper CreateModuleCatalog method override.

2.6 Building a custom module type loader

By using the correct extensibility points we can load our PRISM modules from other sources as well. One such example is loading remote modules by using a web service. Modules are loaded into an application by using the IModuleTypeLoader service. The interface definition can be seen in listing 2.25.

Listing 2.25 – *The IModuleTypeLoader service interface*
```
public interface IModuleTypeLoader
{
    bool CanLoadModuleType(ModuleInfo moduleInfo);
    void LoadModuleType(ModuleInfo moduleInfo);
    event EventHandler<ModuleDownloadProgressChangedEventArgs>
        ModuleDownloadProgressChanged;
    event EventHandler<LoadModuleCompletedEventArgs>
        LoadModuleCompleted;
}
```

The interface exposes 2 methods and 2 events. The events are used to signal download progress and module load termination either successfully or with an error. The CanLoadModuleType method is used to determine if the module loader can be used to load the specified module. The LoadModuleType method is used to potentially download and load the module assembly for the specified module into memory.

The FileModuleTypeLoader is the only WPF implementation offered by PRISM and it is used to load module assemblies from disk. The main work gets done in the LoadModuleType method. Here the Ref property of the ModuleInfo class is analyzed in order to determine the file location on disk. The download progress is set to 0 before the type's assembly is loaded and then it is set to 100. This module type loader is used only for Ref values starting with the 'file://' prefix. After the assembly is loaded into memory its Uri is stored in order to not load it again during the same application run.

The XapModuleTypeLoader implementation is used in Silverlight applications to download remote modules and load them on the client.

In order to download the module assembly from the web service and load it into the application we need to write a custom type loader and make it available to the module manager for use. The module manager exposes a virtual ModuleTypeLoaders property that returns the collection of IModuleTypeLoaders. These type loaders will be used to load the corresponding assemblies into memory before instantiating and initializing the module types.

The following sections describe the steps we need to take in order to create and use our custom IModuleTypeLoader implementation. This sample includes 2 solutions. One solution will contain the module assembly and the WCF service used to return the service to the clients. The second solution will be a WPF PRISM client that will use the custom type loader to load the module returned by the service.

2.6.1 Creating the WCF service

We will keep the service architecture and implementation really simple. The service will be self-hosted inside a console application. Create a new console application project and add the following WCF assembly references: System.ServiceModel.dll and System.Runtime.Serialization.dll. Add the service contract presented in listing 2.26 to this project.

Listing 2.26 – *The WCF service interface definition*
```
[ServiceContract(Name="http://badeaco.com/samples/")]
public interface IModuleService
{
    [OperationContract]
    byte[] GetModule();
}
```

The WCF service will expose a single service method. This method will return the byte array representing the module assembly bytes. Add the implementation of this service as shown in listing 2.27.

Listing 2.27 – *Implementing the WCF service*
```
public class ModuleService:IModuleService
{
    public byte[] GetModule()
    {
        using (var stream =
         new FileStream("Modules/Module3.dll",
         FileMode.Open, FileAccess.Read))
        {
            using (var ms = new MemoryStream())
            {
                byte[] data = new byte[stream.Length];
```

```
            stream.Read(data, 0, data.Length);
            ms.Write(data, 0, data.Length);
            ms.Position = 0;
            return ms.ToArray();
        }
      }
    }
}
```

The service implementation reads the module assembly from the specified path. The assembly is located in the Modules directory under the executable path. The implementation opens a stream and returns the assembly bytes. Modify the Main method as shown in listing 2.28, to host the WCF service.

Listing 2.28 – *Hosting the WCF service in a console application*
```
static void Main(string[] args)
{
    using (var host = new ServiceHost(typeof(ModuleService)))
    {
        Console.WriteLine("Starting service...");
        host.Open();
        Console.WriteLine("Started.\nPress any key to exit...");
        Console.ReadKey();
    }
}
```

Add the service configuration presented in listing 2.29 to the project App.config file.

Listing 2.29 – *The WCF service configuration*
```
<system.serviceModel>
  <services>
    <service name="ModuleLoaderServiceClient.Implementations.ModuleService" behaviorCon
figuration="behavior">
      <host>
        <baseAddresses>
          <add baseAddress="http://localhost:8080/"/>
        </baseAddresses>
      </host>
      <endpoint address="ModuleService" binding="wsHttpBinding"
          contract="ModuleLoaderServiceClient.Interfaces.IModuleService"/>
      <endpoint address="mex" binding="mexHttpBinding"
          contract="IMetadataExchange"/>
    </service>
  </services>
  <behaviors>
    <serviceBehaviors>
      <behavior name="behavior">
        <serviceDebug includeExceptionDetailInFaults="true"/>
        <serviceMetadata httpGetEnabled="true"/>
      </behavior>
    </serviceBehaviors>
```

```xml
        </behaviors>
</system.serviceModel>
```

This is a classic configuration. We expose the service over http using port 8080. Note that your service name and contract name might be different. This depends on your project name and on the namespace in which you added the classes.

Implementing the module
Add a WPF UserControl library project to the existing solution. This library will contain the module definition. Add the Microsoft.Practices.Prism.dll assembly reference in order to use the IModule interface. Add the class definition presented in listing 2.30 to this assembly.

Listing 2.30 – *Implementing the Module3 module. This module will be downloaded through the service*
```csharp
public class Module3:IModule
{
    private IRegionManager regionManager;
    public Module3(IRegionManager regionManager)
    {
        this.regionManager = regionManager;
    }
    public void Initialize()
    {
        regionManager.RegisterViewWithRegion("DemoRegion",
          () => { return "hello from module 3"; });
    }
}
```

This is a simple module implementation. The region manager is injected into the module constructor. We'll use this region manager to register a view with the DemoRegion region. This will be a region in the Shell UI.

Change the build output location for this project in order for it to be found by the service. Figure 2.4 presents the relative path. Note that your path may be different depending on your project name.

Figure 2.4 – *Changing the build output path*

Also make sure you add a dependency on the module project from the service project. To do this, open the solution properties page. Select the Project Dependencies tab and make sure the service project is dependent on the module project as shown in figure 2.5. This will ensure that every time the service project is built, so is the module project.

2.6.2 Building the WPF client
The second solution will contain the WPF application. This application will be a modular application

that will use the custom module type loader to access the service developed previously and load the module.

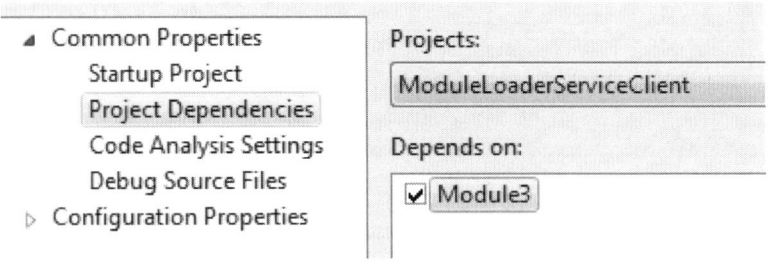

Figure 2.5 – *Setting project dependencies*

Create a new WPF project and add the following PRISM assembly references to this project: Microsoft.Practices.Prism.dll, Microsoft.Practices.Unity.dll, Microsoft.Practices.ServiceLocation.dll and Microsoft.Practices.Prism.UnityExtensions.dll. Add the bootstrapper class definition to the WPF project as shown in listing 2.31.

Listing 2.31 – *The application bootstrapper definition*
```
public class Bootstrapper:UnityBootstrapper
{
    protected override IModuleCatalog CreateModuleCatalog()
    {
        return Microsoft.Practices.Prism.Modularity
          .ModuleCatalog.CreateFromXaml(new Uri(
           "/TypeLoaderSample;component/modules.xaml",
           UriKind.Relative));
    }
    protected override DependencyObject CreateShell()
    {
        return new MainWindow();
    }
    protected override void InitializeShell()
    {
        base.InitializeShell();
        var view = Shell as MainWindow;
        App.Current.MainWindow = view;
        App.Current.MainWindow.Show();
    }
}
```

The application will use a module catalog configured from a XAML file. Add the modules.txt text file to the project but change its extension to .xaml before clicking the Add button. Using a XAML file, you will have the benefit of IntelliSense. If you get parser exceptions you can use a plain txt file to define the catalog. The code shown in listing 2.32 presents the catalog configuration code.

Listing 2.32 – *Defining the module catalog in XAML*
```
<m:ModuleCatalog xmlns="http://schemas.microsoft.com/winfx/2006/xaml/presentation"
```

```xml
xmlns:x="http://schemas.microsoft.com/winfx/2006/xaml" xmlns:m="clr-
namespace:Microsoft.Practices.Prism.Modularity;assembly=Microsoft.Practices.Prism" >
    <m:ModuleInfo ModuleName="Module3"
         Ref="http://localhost:8080/ModuleService"
         ModuleType="Module3.Module3, Module3, Version=1.0.0.0"/>
</m:ModuleCatalog>
```

As you can see from the code in listing 2.32, the Ref attribute is set to the address of the web service. The default FileModuleTypeLoader type loader won't be able to handle this module as its CanLoadModuleType method returns true only if the Ref property value is a file path. Add the following XAML to the Shell view.

```xml
<ItemsControl Grid.Row="1"
        prism:RegionManager.RegionName="DemoRegion">
</ItemsControl>
```

This is a simple ItemsControl that represents the region to which the module will register its view. The last thing we need to do is implement the type loader.

Implementing the custom type loader

Our type loader will call a web service in order to download the module assembly. Before we implement our loader, add a reference to the System.ServiceModel.dll assembly (make sure you also add the IModuleService contract from the service project. We will not use the Add Service Reference wizard.).

Add an IModuleTypeLoader implementataion to your project as shown in listing 2.33.

Listing 2.33 – *Implementing the IModuleTypeLoader interface*
```csharp
public class WebServiceTypeLoader:IModuleTypeLoader
{
    public bool CanLoadModuleType(ModuleInfo moduleInfo)
    {
        throw new NotImplementedException();
    }
    public void LoadModuleType(ModuleInfo moduleInfo)
    {
        throw new NotImplementedException();
    }

    public event EventHandler<LoadModuleCompletedEventArgs>
        LoadModuleCompleted;
    public event EventHandler<
        ModuleDownloadProgressChangedEventArgs>
        ModuleDownloadProgressChanged;
}
```

Add the implementation for the CanLoadModuleType method as shown in listing 2.34. This method will be called by the IModuleManager implementation when it needs to handle module loading. In this method the module type loader will specify if it can handle loading a particular module.

Listing 2.34 – *Determining if the type loader can load the module*
```
public bool CanLoadModuleType(ModuleInfo moduleInfo)
{
    if (moduleInfo == null)
    {
        throw new System.ArgumentNullException("moduleInfo");
    }
    if (moduleInfo.Ref != null &&
        moduleInfo.Ref.ToLower().StartsWith("http://"))
        return true;
    return false;
}
```

You can see, from the code in listing 2.34, that our type loader will handle module loading for all modules for which the Ref property represents a web address. The default implementation checked that the Ref property is a file path. Add the implementation for the LoadModuleType method as shown in listing 2.35. This method will be called to Load the module assembly into memory.

Listing 2.35 – *Loading the module*
```
public void LoadModuleType(ModuleInfo moduleInfo)
{
    if (moduleInfo == null)
    {
        throw new System.ArgumentNullException("moduleInfo");
    }
    IModuleService proxy = ChannelFactory<IModuleService>
        .CreateChannel(new WSHttpBinding(),
            new EndpointAddress(moduleInfo.Ref));
    try
    {
        Uri uri = new Uri(moduleInfo.Ref,
         UriKind.RelativeOrAbsolute);
        if (IsSuccessfullyDownloaded(uri))
        {
            RaiseLoadModuleCompleted(moduleInfo, null);
        }
        else
        {
            RaiseModuleDownloadProgressChanged(moduleInfo, 0, 1);
            byte[] data = proxy.GetModule();
            RaiseModuleDownloadProgressChanged(moduleInfo, 1, 1);

            int idx = moduleInfo.ModuleType.IndexOf(',');
            string str = moduleInfo.ModuleType
                    .Substring(idx + 2);
            var asmInfo = new AssemblyInfo()
            {
                AssemblyUri = uri,
```

```
            AssemblyName = new AssemblyName(str),
            Data = data
        };
        registeredAssemblies.Add(asmInfo);
        this.RecordDownloadSuccess(uri);
        this.RaiseLoadModuleCompleted(moduleInfo, null);
    }
}
catch (Exception ex)
{
    RaiseLoadModuleCompleted(moduleInfo, ex);
}
finally
{
    IDisposable disp = proxy as IDisposable;
    if (disp != null) disp.Dispose();
}
}
```

The first thing this method does it to create a communication channel to the web service by using the value in the Ref property. After this, an Uri is constructed and checked against a local collection. This ensures that we do not try to download the same assembly multiple times. The IsSuccessfullyDownloaded method definition can be seen in listing 2.36.

Listing 2.36 – *Checking if a module has already been downloaded*
```
private HashSet<Uri> downloadedUris = new HashSet<Uri>();
private bool IsSuccessfullyDownloaded(Uri uri)
{
    lock (this.downloadedUris)
    {
        return this.downloadedUris.Contains(uri);
    }
}
```

If the assembly has already been downloaded we just call the LoadModuleCompletedEvent. The method definition can be seen in listing 2.37.

Listing 2.37 – *Raising the LoadModuleCompleted event*
```
private void RaiseLoadModuleCompleted(ModuleInfo moduleInfo,
        Exception error)
{
    if (this.LoadModuleCompleted != null)
    {
        var e = new LoadModuleCompletedEventArgs(moduleInfo,
          error);
        this.LoadModuleCompleted(this, e);
    }
}
```

Next, we trigger the load progress changed event and access the web service to download the data. At the end we trigger the progress changed event again. The method definition can be seen in listing 2.38.

Listing 2.38 – *Notifying the download progress has changed*
```csharp
private void RaiseModuleDownloadProgressChanged(
        ModuleInfo moduleInfo, long bytesReceived,
        long totalBytesToReceive)
{
    if (this.ModuleDownloadProgressChanged != null)
    {
        var e = new ModuleDownloadProgressChangedEventArgs
            (moduleInfo, bytesReceived, totalBytesToReceive);
        this.ModuleDownloadProgressChanged(this, e);
    }
}
```

After the data is downloaded we store it locally in an AssemblyInfo instance. The AssemblyInfo class definition can be seen in listing 2.39.

Listing 2.39 – *Downloaded module information*
```csharp
private class AssemblyInfo
{
    public AssemblyName AssemblyName { get; set; }
    public Uri AssemblyUri { get; set; }
    public Assembly Assembly { get; set; }
    public byte[] Data { get; set; }
}
```

At the end, we record the Uri for later reference and trigger the module loaded event. The method definition can be seen in listing 2.40.

Listing 2.40 – *Recording that a module has been downloaded*
```csharp
private void RecordDownloadSuccess(Uri uri)
{
    lock (this.downloadedUris)
    {
        this.downloadedUris.Add(uri);
    }
}
```

The important code in this class is the subscription to the AppDomain.AssemblyResolve event. This code can be seen in listing 2.41.

Listing 2.41 – *Supplying the module assembly on resolution failure*
```csharp
public WebServiceTypeLoader()
{
    AppDomain.CurrentDomain.AssemblyResolve +=
        this.CurrentDomain_AssemblyResolve;
}
```

```csharp
private Assembly CurrentDomain_AssemblyResolve(object sender,
        ResolveEventArgs args)
{
    AssemblyName assemblyName = new AssemblyName(args.Name);
    AssemblyInfo assemblyInfo = this.registeredAssemblies
        .FirstOrDefault(a => AssemblyName
         .ReferenceMatchesDefinition(
                assemblyName, a.AssemblyName));
    if (assemblyInfo != null)
    {
        if (assemblyInfo.Assembly == null)
            assemblyInfo.Assembly =
                Assembly.Load(assemblyInfo.Data);
        return assemblyInfo.Assembly;
    }
    return null;
}
```

When the module initializer tries to instantiate the module type it will throw an exception because the module assembly has not been loaded yet. This is when the AssemblyResolve event is triggered. The AssemblyResolve event is triggered when the runtime fails to bind to an assembly by name. We subscribe to this event in order to supply the module assembly whenever the resolution fails. When this happens, we look for the assembly in the local collection and load it into the current AppDomain by using the Assembly.Load method. At the end we return the assembly.

The default implementation of the IModuleTypeLoader interface was taken as an example when implementing the WebServiceTypeLoader class.

Integrating the type loader

Now that we have implemented the custom type loader, we need to use it. We do this by adding it to the ModuleTypeLoaders property of the module manager. What we want to do is derive our own module manager class from the default IModuleManager implementation and add our custom type loader to the collection of existing type loaders. This can be seen in listing 2.42.

Listing 2.42 – *Adding the custom type loader to the manager's list of type loaders*
```csharp
public class CustomModuleManager:ModuleManager
{
    public CustomModuleManager(
        IModuleInitializer moduleInitializer,
        IModuleCatalog moduleCatalog, ILoggerFacade loggerFacade)
        : base(moduleInitializer, moduleCatalog, loggerFacade)
    {
        ModuleTypeLoaders = new List<IModuleTypeLoader>()
            {
                new FileModuleTypeLoader(),
                new WebServiceTypeLoader()
            };
    }
}
```

The ModuleTypeLoaders property returns an IEnumerable of IModuleTypeLoader. The only item contained by default, is an instance of the FileModuleTypeLoader type for WPF. Silverlight uses a XapTypeLoader instance. This loader is used to load module assemblies from disk. To determine which type loader is to be used when loading a module assembly, the module manager calls the CanLoadModuleType method defined in the IModuleTypeLoader interface.

The last thing we need to do is to use this module manager instead of the default one. We do this by registering this type before the default registrations are applied. This can be seen in listing 2.43.

Listing 2.43 – *Configuring the container to use the custom module manager*
```
protected override void ConfigureContainer()
{
    Container.RegisterType<IModuleManager, CustomModuleManager>(
        new ContainerControlledLifetimeManager());
    base.ConfigureContainer();
}
```

We can now run the application. Figure 2.6 presents the results. The module is downloaded and the region contains the single view that was registered.

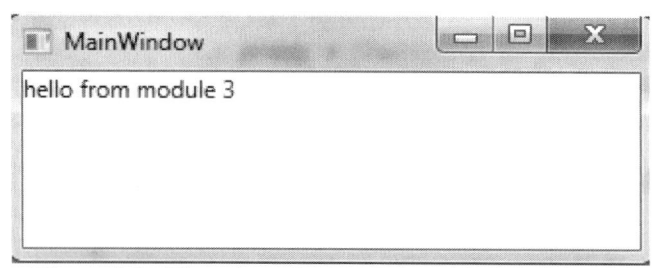

Figure 2.6 – *The main application window with the loaded module*

2.7 Summary

This chapter talked about building modular applications. A module is a logical collection of functionality that can be packaged in one or more assemblies or in a XAP file. All modules have a central class that is used to integrate the module functionality into the application. The application knows about the modules it needs to load by using a module catalog. The module catalog lists all the application modules, their dependencies and their initialization mode.

Module catalogs can be configured in a number of ways depending on the technology that is used. For Silverlight applications, modules can be added by using hard references as well as by using a xaml file. For WPF applications we can also use a configuration file or directory sweeping. PRISM also allows us to load modules from other sources by implementing a custom content type loader.

The module loading process is handled by a module manager. The module manager loads the modules specified in the module catalog at the end of the bootstrapping sequence, immediately after the shell is displayed.

CHAPTER 3: THE MVVM DESIGN PATTERN

The Model-View-ViewModel pattern is a separation design pattern. It allows developers and designers to work on the same application at the same time. The pattern does this by separating the application user interface logic from the business and presentation logic. This separation makes it easier for developers to test, maintain and extend the application.

The MVVM pattern is a specialization of the Presentation Model pattern that takes advantage of the powerful data binding engine provided by WPF and Silverlight. This pattern was specifically designed to be used with these 2 technologies.

The MVVM pattern groups UI, business and presentation logic code into 3 classes: the model (contains the business code), the view (contains the UI code) and the view-model (contains the presentation code). The next section describes these classes in more detail.

3.1 MVVM components

The view

The view represents the application user interface. This is the part of the application that can be seen by the user. Users interact with the application by using its view. The view is usually represented by a Control or UserControl derived class. The view defines the UI elements and their position on the screen. In WPF and Silverlight the view is implemented in a declarative way by using XAML.

The view also has an associated code-behind file that can be used to define UI interaction code. The code-behind file should not contain any business code. It should only contain code that handles particular cases of user interaction. These may include code that starts animations that are difficult to express in XAML or code that directly manipulates UI elements. Most of the time, code in the code-behind file can be moved into behaviors. This leaves the code-behind file almost empty.

Views can also be represented by data templates. These are pieces of XAML that specify how a particular piece of data should be displayed. You can think of a data template as a view without a code behind file. Data templates are usually declared as resources and are referenced from other controls (ContentControl and ItemsControl derived classes).

The view exposes a DataContext property. This property is used to link the view to the view-model. The DataContext property is of type object so there is loose coupling between the view and the view model. The view displays the application data by using data binding. The view controls data bind to properties on the view model in order to display their values.

The model

The model is a non-visual class that represents the application business logic and data. The model classes represent the data that needs to be displayed by the application. Business logic code is also contained in the model and refers to any piece of code that retrieves or manipulates the model data. This can include validation code or code that retrieves the data from a web service or database. The model defines data structures according to the client application domain.

The model is self-contained. It has no knowledge of the view or view-model classes. The model classes usually implement features that make them easier to data bind to the view. These features include change notification events and data validation. Change notification is done by implementing the INotifyPropertyChanged and INotifycollectionChanged interfaces. Data validation is done by implementing the IDataErrorInfo and INotifyDataErrorInfo interfaces.

If the model does not implement the required interfaces, it needs to be adapted in order to obtain the required behavior. This can be done by encapsulating a model class in a view-model. The view-model will implement the required interfaces and will delegate some responsibilities to the contained model.

The view-model

The view-model is a non visual class that encapsulates the presentation logic. The view-model is responsible for coordinating the interactions between the view and the model. There are times when the data that needs to be displayed is too complex to bind directly to the view. A view-model can be used in this case to adapt the model in order to be easily displayed by the view.

The view-model can also encapsulate the view state. This may be represented by a busy state, for example. If the data takes longer to load, the view-model can set a busy flag. This state can then be represented in the view by displaying a piece of UI that blocks user interaction while at the same time informing the user that an operation is currently executing. The view-model usually implements the relevant change notification and data validation interfaces.

The view-model can be tested independently of the view and the model. The view-model has no knowledge of the view classes. Typically the view-model will define commands and actions that can be triggered from the view. The view will represent these commands by using links, buttons or menu items. The view-model will be linked to the view via the view's DataContext property. The view will display the view-model data by using UI controls that will data bind to the properties exposed by the view-model.

3.2 MVVM Class interactions

A successful implementation of the MVVM pattern has 2 parts. The first part is concerned with putting the functionality into the correct classes. The previous section talked about each class's responsibilities. The second part is concerned with the interaction between the MVVM components. Figure 3.1 presents the MVVM class interactions as well as the mechanisms that facilitate it.

The view model is the only one that knows about the model. The view-model retrieves the application data from a web service or from the database. It is its responsibility to modify the model data in order for it to be easily presented in the view. The view-model also saves the potential changes to the store.

The view-model is linked to the view via the view's DataContext property. The UI controls in the view are data bound to the view-model properties. The view-model exposes the necessary properties in order to display the model. Changes in the view-model properties are reflected in the UI by using change notification events. The view-model implements the INotifyPropertyChanged interface. When its properties change, the view-model triggers the PropertyChanged event. The data binding engine automatically subscribes to this event and refreshes the target controls every time the event is triggered in the view-model. User actions in the view are handled in the view-model by using commands. Buttons and menu items are data bound to command objects in the view-model. When the user presses a button the command handlers in the view-model are executed.

The following sections describe the components needed to implement the MVVM pattern successfully in more details. In order to present these components we will implement a customer management application. Before we start building the application there is one more topic I would like to talk about and this concerns instantiating the MVVM classes.

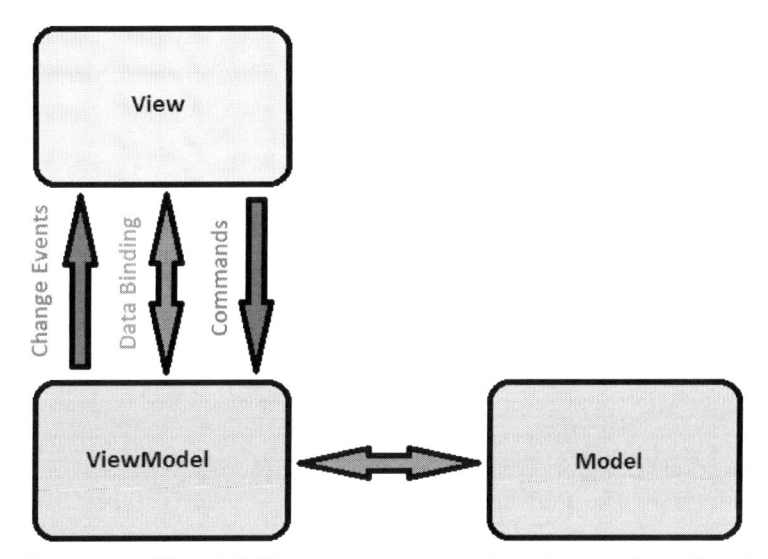

Figure 3.1 – *The MVVM class interactions and the mechanisms that facilitate it*

3.3 Instantiating the view and view-model classes

The MVVM pattern helps you to cleanly separate your UI from your presentation and business logic and data, so implementing the right code in the right class is an important first step in using the MVVM pattern effectively. Managing the interactions between the view and view model classes through data binding and commands is also important aspect to consider. The next step is to consider how the view, view model, and model classes are instantiated and associated with each other at run time.

One option is to link the view and view-model in XAML. This approach means that the view-model needs to have a default constructor. If the view-model has dependencies on other services this approach cannot be used. The code shown in listing 3.1 presents an example.

Listing 3.1 – *Instantiating the view-model in the view XAML*
```xml
<UserControl.DataContext>
    <loc:CustomersViewModel/>
</UserControl.DataContext>
```

Another option would be to link the view-model in the view's code behind. This option is a little more flexible because it allows us to instantiate a view-model even if it has dependencies on other services. The code shown in listing 3.2 presents an example.

Listing 3.2 – *Instantiating the view-model in the view's code-behind*
```csharp
public MainPage()
{
    InitializeComponent();
    ICustomerService service = new CustomerService();
    CustomersViewModel vm = new CustomersViewModel(service);
    DataContext = vm;
}
```

Another option of linking the view and view-model in code is to use constructor injection. This option can be used in conjunction with a dependency injection container. One example of when we might use this approach is when using the PRISM navigation feature with a view first approach. In this situation the views are resolved from a DI container. The code shown in listing 3.3 presents an example.

Listing 3.3 – *Injecting the view-model using constructor injection*
```csharp
public MainPage(CustomersViewModel customersVM)
{
    InitializeComponent();
    DataContext = customersVM;
}
```

Another option of linking the view with the view-model is to use data templates. This method has the advantage of decoupling the 2 components. Data templates are mainly used to specify how list elements are displayed. In this case the DataTemplate will be used to create the view and assign the view-model to the view's DataContext property. The XAML shown in listing 3.4 presents an example.

Listing 3.4 – *Using data templates to display the view-models*
```xml
<ListBox ItemsSource="{Binding Customers}"
         SelectedItem="{Binding Customer, Mode=TwoWay}">
    <ListBox.ItemTemplate>
        <DataTemplate>
            <StackPanel>
                <StackPanel Orientation="Horizontal">
                    <TextBlock Text="{Binding FirstName}"/>
                    <TextBlock Text="{Binding LastName}"/>
                </StackPanel>
                <TextBlock Text="{Binding Age}" />
            </StackPanel>
```

```xml
        </DataTemplate>
    </ListBox.ItemTemplate>
</ListBox>
```

If we want to reuse the DataTemplate multiple times in the same page or window we can create it as a resource. The code presented in listing 3.5 shows this option.

Listing 3.5 – *Reusing data templates by converting them into resources*
```xml
<UserControl.Resources>
    <DataTemplate DataType="loc:Customer">
        <StackPanel>
            <StackPanel Orientation="Horizontal">
                <TextBlock Text="{Binding FirstName}"/>
                <TextBlock Text="{Binding LastName}"/>
            </StackPanel>
            <TextBlock Text="{Binding Age}" />
        </StackPanel>
    </DataTemplate>
</UserControl.Resources>
<ListBox ItemsSource="{Binding Customers}"
         SelectedItem="{Binding Customer, Mode=TwoWay}"/>
```

The automatic data template feature presented here is provided by WPF and Silverlight 5. There is no need here to specify a value for the ItemTemplate property in the ListBox control. An automatically applied data template is also a good solution if we want to display multiple view-model types in the same ContentControl instance. One such example is an application that changes its main work area based on user selection in a control panel.

For applications that have a relatively small number of views and view-models, a view-model locator pattern can be used. In this pattern the ViewModelLocator class can be used to expose view-model properties. The view-model will be bound to the view's DataContext property in the view's XAML by using a binding expression. This allows us to also use view-models without a default constructor. We can use view-models that use constructor injection to inject dependencies. The ViewModelLocator pattern is most commonly used for building Windows Phone applications.

Finally, if you use some kind of dependency injection container, you can use that to create your view and view model classes. Often, you will find it useful to provide a controller or service class that will coordinate the instantiation of the view and view-model. This class can be used in conjunction with the dependency injection container.

3.4 Implementing an MVVM application

The application we are going to build, to show how to implement the MVVM pattern, is a Silverlight application and will allow us to add, edit and delete customers. Figure 3.2 presents the finished application.

The model

The first thing we need to do is to decide the on the application model. Since we want to build a customer management interface we need to model the customer entity. Create a Model folder in the Silverlight application project and add the class definition presented in listing 3.6 to this folder.

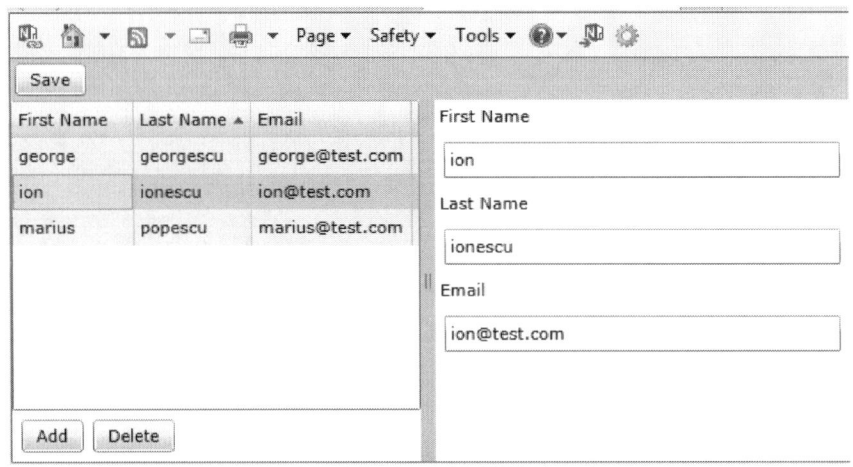

Figure 3.2 – *The finished MVVM application*

Listing 3.6 – *The Customer class definition*
```
public class Customer
{
    public string FirstName { get; set; }
    public string LastName { get; set; }
    public string Email { get; set; }
}
```

In order to read the customer data and to simulate a save operation, we will create and consume a customer service. This is a simple in-memory service that will be injected as a dependency (using constructor injection) into our main view-model class. Add the service interface definition presented in listing 3.7 to the Model folder.

Listing 3.7 – *The customer service interface definition*
```
public interface ICustomerService
{
    List<Customer> GetAll();
    void Save(List<Customer> customers,
        Action<Exception> callback);
}
```

This interface can abstract a web service at some point, but for our example we are going to implement this interface by generating the customer data and holding it in memory. Listing 3.8 presents the implementation for this interface and this needs to be added to the Model directory of the Silverlight project.

Listing 3.8 – *The customer service implementation*
```
public class CustomerService:ICustomerService
{
    private List<Customer> customers;
```

```csharp
public List<Customer> GetAll()
{
    if (customers == null) InitCustomers();
    return customers;
}
private void InitCustomers()
{
    customers = new List<Customer>() {
    new Customer(){FirstName="ion", LastName="ionescu",
        Email="ion@test.com"},
    new Customer(){FirstName="george", LastName="georgescu",
        Email="george@test.com"},
    new Customer(){FirstName="marius", LastName="popescu",
        Email="marius@test.com"},
    };
}
public void Save(List<Customer> customers,
    Action<Exception> callback)
{
    Task.Factory.StartNew(() => {
        Thread.Sleep(3000);
        if(callback!=null)
            Deployment.Current.Dispatcher.BeginInvoke(
                () => { callback(null); });
    });
}
}
```

As you can see, the service will return 3 hardcoded customer entities. Also, the save code will fake a long running asynchronous operation.

Data binding

WPF and Silverlight data binding provides a simple and consistent way for applications to present and interact with their data. Elements can be bound to data from a variety of data sources in the form of CLR objects and XML.

The data binding functionality in WPF and Silverlight has several advantages over traditional models, including a broad range of properties that inherently support data binding, flexible UI representation of data and clean separation of business logic from UI.

Data binding is the process that establishes a connection between the application UI and its business logic. If the binding has the correct settings and the data provides the proper notifications, then, when the data changes its value, the elements that are bound to the data reflect changes automatically. Data binding can also mean that if an outer representation of the data in an element changes, then the underlying data can be automatically updated to reflect the change. For example, if the user edits the value in a TextBox element, the underlying data value is automatically updated to reflect that change.

A typical use of data binding is to place server or local configuration data into forms or other UI controls. In WPF and Silverlight, this concept is expanded to include the binding of a broad range of properties to a variety of data sources. In WPF and Silverlight, dependency properties of elements can be bound to CLR objects (including ADO.NET objects or objects associated with Web Services and Web properties) and XML data.

Binding a UI control to a data source can be done by using the Binding markup expression. The code below shows an example. In this example a TextBox control is bound to a property in the view-model.

```
<TextBox Text="{Binding Path=FirstName, Mode=TwoWay,
    UpdateSourceTrigger=PropertyChanged}" />
```

In this example, we notice that the TextBox will display the value of the FirstName property. This property is read from the binding source. Since the source isn't explicitly specified, the binding looks at the TextBox's DataContext property. When it doesn't find anything it looks at the parent's DataContext and so on.

The Binding presented in the example also sets the communication direction by setting the Mode property. Possible values include: OneWay, OneTime, TwoWay and OneWayToSource (WPF only). The binding in this example is bidirectional. This means that changes to the FirstName property, in code, will automatically update the TextBox control. Also, if the user modifies the TextBox data, the change will be propagated to the FirstName property.

For some control properties, the binding source isn't updated automatically. This is mainly because of performance issues. One example is the TextBox control's Text property. It is assumed that when the user starts typing into the TextBox, a lot of characters will be inserted. Updating the binding source multiple times in rapid succession may pose a performance problem. This is why, by default, for the Text property, the binding source is updated when the TextBox loses focus. In our example we want the FirstName property to be updated every time the text changes. This is why we set the binding's UpdateSourceTrigger property to PropertyChanged. The possible values for the UpdateSourceTrigger binding property are: Default, LostFocus (WPF only), Explicit and PropertyChanged.

This section presented only an overview of data binding features available in WPF and Silverlight. If you want to find out more about this subject you can check out additional resources on the web.

The Views

Our customer management application will be composed of 2 views. One view will be used to display the list of customers and the other will be used to display the customer details. The views will have no knowledge of the view-models. They will use data binding in order to display the data. Add a Views folder to the Silverlight project and add a new Silverlight user control item to this folder. Name the item CustomerView. The XAML shown in listing 3.9 presents this view's content.

Listing 3.9 – *The customer details view definition*
```
<StackPanel>
    <TextBlock Text="First Name"/>
    <TextBox Text="{Binding FirstName, Mode=TwoWay,
        UpdateSourceTrigger=PropertyChanged,
        ValidatesOnNotifyDataErrors=True}" />
    <TextBlock Text="Last Name"/>
    <TextBox Text="{Binding LastName, Mode=TwoWay,
```

```xml
        UpdateSourceTrigger=PropertyChanged,
        ValidatesOnNotifyDataErrors=True}" />
    <TextBlock Text="Email"/>
    <TextBox Text="{Binding Email, Mode=TwoWay,
        UpdateSourceTrigger=PropertyChanged,
        ValidatesOnNotifyDataErrors=True}" />
</StackPanel>
```

Add another Silverlight user control item to the View folder. Name this item CustomerListView. This user control will be used to display the list of customers. The XAML shown in listing 3.10 presents the view's content.

Listing 3.10 – *The customer list view definition*
```xml
<Grid x:Name="LayoutRoot" Background="White">
    <Grid.RowDefinitions>
        <RowDefinition Height="*"/>
        <RowDefinition Height="auto"/>
    </Grid.RowDefinitions>
    <sdk:DataGrid ItemsSource="{Binding Customers}"
            SelectedItem="{Binding SelectedCustomer, Mode=TwoWay}"
            IsReadOnly="True" AutoGenerateColumns="False">
        <sdk:DataGrid.Columns>
            <sdk:DataGridTextColumn Header="First Name"
                    Binding="{Binding FirstName}" />
            <sdk:DataGridTextColumn Header="Last Name" Binding="{Binding LastName}"/>
            <sdk:DataGridTextColumn Header="Email" Binding="{Binding Email}"/>
        </sdk:DataGrid.Columns>
    </sdk:DataGrid>
    <StackPanel Orientation="Horizontal" Grid.Row="1" Margin="3">
        <Button Content="Add" Command="{Binding AddCommand}"/>
        <Button Content="Delete"
          Command="{Binding DeleteCommand}"/>
    </StackPanel>
</Grid>
```

You can see that we have a DataGrid control that we use to display the customer list. We made the DataGrid read-only and we also specified that we don't want the control to generate our columns for us. We manually defined the 3 columns in order to display the customer data. The DataGrid is bound to two view-model properties. It is bound to the Customers property in order to know what list to display. It is also bound to the SelectedCustomer property in order to store the currently selected customer. This is important as we need to determine the customer we want to delete. At the bottom we have 2 buttons that are bound to the Add and Delete commands.

These two views are brought together in the MainPage. The XAML shown in listing 3.11 presents the main page content.

Listing 3.11 – *The application's MainPage view definition*
```xml
<Grid x:Name="LayoutRoot" Background="White">
    <Grid.RowDefinitions>
        <RowDefinition Height="auto"/>
```

```xml
            <RowDefinition Height="*"/>
        </Grid.RowDefinitions>
        <Button Content="Save" Command="{Binding SaveCommand}"
            HorizontalAlignment="Left" />
        <Grid Grid.Row="1">
            <Grid.ColumnDefinitions>
                <ColumnDefinition Width="*"/>
                <ColumnDefinition Width="auto"/>
                <ColumnDefinition Width="*"/>
            </Grid.ColumnDefinitions>
            <ContentControl HorizontalContentAlignment="Stretch"
                    VerticalContentAlignment="Stretch" Content="{Binding}">
                <ContentControl.ContentTemplate>
                    <DataTemplate>
                        <view:CustomerListView />
                    </DataTemplate>
                </ContentControl.ContentTemplate>
            </ContentControl>
            <sdk:GridSplitter Grid.Column="1" HorizontalAlignment="Stretch"
                    VerticalAlignment="Stretch" Width="10" />
            <ContentControl Grid.Column="2" Content="{Binding SelectedCustomer}"
                    HorizontalContentAlignment="Stretch">
                <ContentControl.ContentTemplate>
                    <DataTemplate>
                        <view:CustomerView />
                    </DataTemplate>
                </ContentControl.ContentTemplate>
            </ContentControl>
        </Grid>
        <Border Background="#33000000" Grid.RowSpan="2" Visibility="{Binding Visible}">
            <Border BorderThickness="1" BorderBrush="Black"
              Padding="5" Background="White"
              HorizontalAlignment="Center" VerticalAlignment="Center">
                <StackPanel>
                    <TextBlock Text="Loading..." Margin="2"/>
                    <ProgressBar IsIndeterminate="{Binding IsBusy}"
                            Width="100" Height="20" Margin="2"/>
                </StackPanel>
            </Border>
        </Border>
    </Grid>
```

At the top of the page we have the save button. This button is data bound to the SaveCommand property in the main view-model class. The customer list is placed on the left while the details are placed on the right. We use ContentControl instances with appropriately defined data templates in order to present the content. You can see that the content control that presents the list of customers is bound to the entire data context in order to have access to the main view-model instance. The second content control is bound to the selected customer.

At the bottom of the screen we have a piece of UI that is shown when the application is busy. In order to do this we bind the Border.Visibility property to the view-model's Visible property. Also the progress bar IsIndeterminate property is bound to the view-model IsDirty flag in order to conserve the processor while the view is not shown.

Change notification events

Change notification events are important if we want the UI to refresh itself every time a property changes in the view-model. The change events tell the binding engine to refresh the UI control that is the target of the binding. The data binding engines in WPF and Silverlight automatically subscribe to the INotifyPropertyChanged and INotifyCollectionChanged events. The INotifyPropertyChanged interface can be implemented if we want to notify other code when the properties in our view-model change. The interface definition is presented in listing 3.12.

Listing 3.12 – *The INotifyPropertyChanged interface definition*
```
public interface INotifyPropertyChanged
{
    event PropertyChangedEventHandler PropertyChanged;
}
```

The interface exposes a single event. This event should be raised after a property value changes. Raising this event in a view-model with multiple properties can result in a lot of duplicate code. For this reason this interface is usually implemented in a base class. Derived classes call a base class method to trigger the event after every property change. The code shown in listing 3.13 presents the base class definition.

Listing 3.13 – *Implementing the change notification interface in a base class*
```
public class InpcBase : INotifyPropertyChanged
{
    protected void NotifyChanged(string name)
    {
        if (PropertyChanged != null)
            PropertyChanged(this,
                new PropertyChangedEventArgs(name));
    }
    public event PropertyChangedEventHandler PropertyChanged;
}
```

The PRISM library also offers such a base class that implements the INotifyPropertyChanged interface. This is the NotificationObject class. This class also offers some helper methods that allow us to trigger the Propertychanged event in a strongly typed manner.

The implementations presented so far trigger the event by specifying the property name with a string. This can produce errors later on if we decide to refactor the code and rename the properties. The NotificationObject class offered by PRISM allows us to trigger the event by specifying the property name as a lambda expression.

Create the ViewModels folder in the Silverlight project and add the definition for the CustomerViewModel class as shown in listing 3.14.

Listing 3.14 – *The customer details view-model definition*
```
public class CustomerViewModel : NotificationObject
{
```

```
    private Customer customer;
    public CustomerViewModel(Customer customer)
    {
        if (customer == null)
          throw new ArgumentNullException("customer");
        this.customer = customer;
    }
    public Customer Customer { get { return customer; } }
    public string FirstName
    {
        get { return customer.FirstName; }
        set
        {
            if (customer.FirstName == value) return;
            customer.FirstName = value;
            RaisePropertyChanged(()=>FirstName);
        }
    }
    public string LastName
    {
        get { return customer.LastName; }
        set
        {
            if (customer.LastName == value) return;
            customer.LastName = value;
            RaisePropertyChanged(()=>LastName);
        }
    }
    public string Email
    {
        get { return customer.Email; }
        set
        {
            if (customer.Email == value) return;
            customer.Email = value;
            RaisePropertyChanged(()=>Email);
        }
    }
}
```

You can see that the CustomerViewModel class accepts a Customer entity as a constructor argument. If we look at the NotificationObject implementation we can see that the functionality we are interested in is exposed by the PropertySupport class. This class exposes a static method that uses the expression passed as an argument to obtain a property name. The NotificationObject code, for this, can be seen in listing 3.15.

Listing 3.15 – *Raising the PropertyChanged event in the NotificationObject class*
```
protected void RaisePropertyChanged<T>(
        Expression<Func<T>> propertyExpression)
{
    var propertyName = PropertySupport
```

```csharp
            .ExtractPropertyName(propertyExpression);
    this.RaisePropertyChanged(propertyName);
}
```

The INotifyCollectionChanged interface can be used to notify subscribers if a collection changes. The interface definition can be seen in listing 3.16.

Listing 3.16 – *The INotifyCollectionChanged interface definition*
```csharp
public interface INotifyCollectionChanged
{
    event NotifyCollectionChangedEventHandler CollectionChanged;
}
```

The CollectionChanged event should be triggered every time the collection changes. This includes: adding items, removing items, moving items, replacing items and resetting the collection. Implementing this interface is not a trivial undertaking. Fortunately for us there is an implementation of this interface in the .NET framework. Instead of implementing this interface we can use the ObservableCollection<T> class. Add the definition presented in listing 3.17, to the ViewModels folder, for the CustomersViewModel class.

Listing 3.17 – *The customers list view-model definition*
```csharp
public class CustomersViewModel : NotificationObject
{
    private ObservableCollection<CustomerViewModel> customers;
    private CustomerViewModel selCustomer;
    private ICustomerService custService;
    private bool isBusy;
    public CustomersViewModel(ICustomerService customerService)
    {
        custService = customerService;
    }

    public bool IsBusy
    {
        get { return isBusy; }
        set
        {
            if (isBusy == value) return;
            isBusy = value;
            RaisePropertyChanged("IsBusy");
            RaisePropertyChanged("Visible");
        }
    }
    public Visibility Visible
    {
        get { return IsBusy ?
          Visibility.Visible : Visibility.Collapsed; }
    }
    public CustomerViewModel SelectedCustomer
    {
```

```
        get { return selCustomer; }
        set
        {
            if (selCustomer == value) return;
            selCustomer = value;
            RaisePropertyChanged("SelectedCustomer");
        }
    }
    public ObservableCollection<CustomerViewModel> Customers
    {
        get
        {
            if (customers == null) GetCustomers();
            return customers;
        }
        private set
        {
            if (customers == value) return;
            customers = value;
            RaisePropertyChanged("Customers");
        }
    }
    private void GetCustomers()
    {
        var res = custService.GetAll();
        Customers = new ObservableCollection<CustomerViewModel>(
            res.Select(p => new CustomerViewModel(p)));
    }
}
```

By using an ObservableCollection<CustomerViewModel> instance we can add elements to the collection in code and have the UI automatically refresh to reflect the changes. In order to run the application we need to link the CustomersViewModel view-model to the main UI. Add the code presented in listing 3.18 to the Application_Startup event handler located in the App.xaml.cs file.

Listing 3.18 – *Linking the view-model with the main UI*
```
private void Application_Startup(object sender,
         StartupEventArgs e)
{
    ICustomerService service = new CustomerService();
    CustomersViewModel vm = new CustomersViewModel(service);
    MainPage view = new MainPage();
    view.DataContext = vm;
    this.RootVisual = view;
}
```

At this point you should be able to run the application and retrieve the list of customers. The buttons won't work yet since we didn't add the commands.

Things get a little more complicated if we also want to sort, group and filter the collection data. In these cases we can use the CollectionViewSource (for WPF) and PagedCollectionView (for

Silverlight) classes.

Implementing ICollectionView

In WPF, when you bind a collection to an ItemsControl, a data view is created behind the scenes. This view is the one that gets bound to the control. This data view is a window into your data source. It tracks the currently selected item and allows you to implement sorting, filtering and grouping. The type of data view that gets created depends on the data source, but the following options are available in WPF: CollectionView, ListCollectionView and BindingListCollectionView.

The CollectionView view type is created if your data source implements the IEnumerable interface. This is the base class for the other data view classes. The ListCollectionView view type is created if your data source implements the IList interface. ListCollectionView derives from CollectionView. The BindingListCollectionView view type is created if your data source implements IBIndingList. BindingListCollectionView derives from CollectionView.

All these classes implement the ICollectionView interface and you can think of them a view-models that allow you to further manipulate the data that gets displayed. If you want to add the functionality offered by these view types to your WPF application, you need to use the CollectionViewSource class. This class has a static method, GetDefaultView, which can be used to retrieve the default data view for your data source.

For Silverlight we will use the PagedCollectionView class. In addition to the presented functionality, this class also allows us to page the data. Add the following private field to the CustomersViewModel class definition. What we want to do is to populate this paged collection view and expose it to the view.

```
private PagedCollectionView pagedCustomers;
```

Modify the GetCustomers method as shown in listing 3.19, in order to instantiate this new private filed.

Listing 3.19 – *Sorting customers by using an ICollectionView implementation*
```
private void GetCustomers()
{
    var res = custService.GetAll();
    customers = new ObservableCollection<CustomerViewModel>(
        res.Select(p => new CustomerViewModel(p)));
    Customers = new PagedCollectionView(customers);
    Customers.SortDescriptions.Add(
        new SortDescription("LastName",
          ListSortDirection.Ascending));
}
```

Modify the Customers property as well, in order to expose the PagedCollectionView instance. The code presented in listing 3.20 shows the changes.

Listing 3.20 – *Exposing the PagedCollectionView for data-binding*
```
public PagedCollectionView Customers
{
    get
```

```
    {
        if (customers == null) GetCustomers();
            return pagedCustomers;
    }
    private set
    {
        if (pagedCustomers == value) return;
        pagedCustomers = value;
        RaisePropertyChanged("Customers");
    }
}
```

This implementation is almost the same to the previous one, but now we can do a lot more things with our collection. As the previous code shows, we also added a sort description in order to sort the customers in ascending order by their last name.

Grouping can be done by using the PagedCollectionView's GroupDescriptions property. This property represents a collection of GroupDescription instances. WPF and Silverlight offer a single implementation of this abstract class in the form of the PropertyGroupDescription class. One interesting thing to note here is that we can group objects even by properties that are not immediately obvious. One such example is grouping by age intervals.

In order to filter our data we need to set the ICollectionView.Filter property. This property needs a Predicate<object> delegate that points to the filter method. Item tracking can be done by using the CurrentItem property. We also have the possibility to navigate the collection in code by using appropriate methods exposed by the ICollectionView interface. These are methods such as: MoveCurrentToFirst, MoveCurrentToNext, etc.

Commands

Commands are used to separate the semantics and object that invokes the command from the logic that executes the command. This allows us to invoke a command by using multiple command sources and also allows us to customize the command logic for different command targets. One example is the Save command. In an application the user might invoke the Save command by using a menu option, a toolbar button or the Ctrl+S key combination. All these sources can be linked to the same command in order to prevent code duplication.

One other purpose for commands is to present the availability of an operation. An example of this would be that if a document isn't modified the Save command shouldn't be available. Once the document is dirty the command becomes available and the user can save the data.

In MVVM, commands are used in order to respond to user actions in the view. A view-model will expose a command property and a UI element in the view will bind to that property. When the UI element is pressed, the command will be invoked and the view-model code will execute the required action.

In WPF and Silverlight, commands are represented by the ICommand interface. The interface definition can be seen in listing 3.21.

Listing 3.21 – *The ICommand interface definition*
```
public interface ICommand
{
    event EventHandler CanExecuteChanged;
```

```
    bool CanExecute(object parameter);
    void Execute(object parameter);
}
```

The Execute method defines the code that should execute when the command is invoked. The CanExecute method defines the code that determines whether the command can execute in its current state. The CanExecutechanged event is triggered when changes appear that affect whether or not the command should execute.

Silverlight doesn't provide any ICommand implementations, so we need to provide our own implementation when writing Sliveright applications that use the MVVM pattern. RoutedCommand and RoutedUICommand are the two WPF implementations of the ICommand interface. These two implementations do not contain the code that will execute the commands. Instead the Execute and CanExecute implementations in these classes raise events that traverse the element tree in search of a CommandBinding object. The handlers that are attached to the CommandBinding are the ones that execute the command.

This implementation is not MVVM friendly. This is why MVVM WPF applications use a custom ICommand implementation, just like in Silverlight.

Having an ICommand implementation for every command can be a little difficult to maintain. This is why a popular ICommand implementation is to use delegates. In this way the view-models can define the command handlers in the same place as the command properties they expose. When the commands are invoked, the handlers in the view-model will execute the command logic. One such implementation is the RelayCommand. The code for this class can be seen in listing 3.22.

Listing 3.22 – *Implementing the ICommand interface*
```
public class RelayCommand:ICommand
{
    private Action execute;
    private Func<bool> canExecute;
    public RelayCommand(Action execute,
        Func<bool> canExecute=null)
    {
        if (execute == null)
            throw new ArgumentNullException("execute");
        this.execute = execute;
        this.canExecute = canExecute;
    }
    public bool CanExecute(object parameter)
    {
        if (canExecute == null) return true;
        return canExecute();
    }
    public event EventHandler CanExecuteChanged;
    public void Execute(object parameter)
    {
        if (CanExecute(parameter))
            execute();
    }
    public void RaiseCanExecuteChanged()
    {
```

```csharp
        if (CanExecuteChanged != null)
            CanExecuteChanged(this, EventArgs.Empty);
    }
}
```

You can see that, in the constructor, the command accepts the methods that will execute the command. These methods are passed by using delegates. When the UI element that is linked to the command checks to see if the command should execute, it calls the ICommand.CanExecute method. This, in turn, calls the canExecute delegate. If the delegate returns false the control will disable itself. When the command needs to execute, it will call the execute delegate.

The UI element that is linked to the command knows to check for the command state by subscribing to the CanExecuteChanged event. When this event is triggered, the UI element calls the command CanExecute method. The RelayCommand implementation also exposes a method that allows us to trigger the CanExecuteChanged event explicitly. This is in order to provide a uniform implementation for both WPF and Silverlight. We can call this method when the view-model state changes, in order to refresh the command states in the view.

We do not need to provide our own ICommand implementation when using the PRISM library. PRISM offers its own implementation of ICommand in the form of the DelegateCommand class. This class has a similar implementation and usage pattern to the RelayCommand class. It also offers additional benefits in the form of an active state.

PRISM also provides a CompositeCommand class. This is an ICommand implementation that allows us to execute multiple commands at the same time. If command monitoring is enabled, we can execute only the active commands that are registered with the CompositeCommand instance. We will cover the DelegateCommand and CompositeCommand classes in more detail in a later chapter.

Add the command definitions and initialization code presented in listing 3.23 to the CustomersViewModel class. These are the definitions for the 3 commands we are supporting in our application.

Listing 3.23 – *Application command definitions*
```csharp
private DelegateCommand saveCmd, addCmd, delCmd;
public CustomersViewModel(ICustomerService customerService)
{
    custService = customerService;
    saveCmd = new DelegateCommand(OnSave);
    addCmd = new DelegateCommand(OnAdd);
    delCmd = new DelegateCommand(OnDelete, CanDelete);
}
```

The code in listing 3.24 presents the command properties and their handlers. The delete command can execute only if a customer is currently selected. The save handler sets the IsBusy property to true before invoking the Save service method. When the method returns the property is set to false again in order to hide the progress indicator.

Listing 3.24 – *Defining the command properties and handlers*
```csharp
public DelegateCommand SaveCommand { get { return saveCmd; } }
public DelegateCommand AddCommand { get { return addCmd; } }
public DelegateCommand DeleteCommand { get { return delCmd; } }
```

```csharp
private void OnSave()
{
    IsBusy = true;
    custService.Save(customers.Select(p => p.Customer).ToList(), ex => {
        IsBusy = false;
    });
}
private void OnAdd()
{
    var vm = new CustomerViewModel(new Customer());
    customers.Add(vm); SelectedCustomer = vm;
}
private void OnDelete() { Customers.Remove(SelectedCustomer); }
private bool CanDelete() { return SelectedCustomer != null; }
```

Since the delete command should only work when a customer is selected, we should invalidate the command in the SelectedCustomer setter. The code presented in listing 3.25 shows how this is done.

Listing 3.25 – *Invalidating the delete command*
```csharp
set
{
    if (selCustomer == value) return;
    selCustomer = value;
    RaisePropertyChanged("SelectedCustomer");
    delCmd.RaiseCanExecuteChanged();
}
```

Running the application at this point will allow us to work with customers in memory. We can add, edit and remove customers.

Another option of executing code when the user interacts with the view, is to use command methods. These are normal methods exposed by the view-model. In the view, we use TriggerActions to invoke the methods when an element triggers a particular event. This was a common pattern in older Silverlight versions that didn't expose ICommand properties from UI elements. The command method pattern can also be used when we want to execute code when various UI events, other then Click, are triggered.

The XAML in listing 3.26 presents an example of invoking a command method when the click event is triggered on a button. The code uses the CallMethodAction trigger action.

Listing 3.26 – *Invoking a command by using a trigger action*
```xml
<Button Content="Save">
    <i:Interaction.Triggers>
        <i:EventTrigger EventName="Click">
            <ei:CallMethodAction MethodName="Save" TargetObject="{Binding}" />
        </i:EventTrigger>
    </i:Interaction.Triggers>
</Button>
```

The method name is specified in the MethodName property. The instance on which to execute the method is specified by using the TargetObject property. In this case, since the target object is the view-model, we use the binding expression with no additional parameters. Before you use the CallMethodAction trigger action make sure to add references to the System.Windows.Interactivity.dll and the Microsoft.Expression.Interactions.dll assemblies. Also add the namespace prefix definitions to the XAML file. The code in listing 3.27 presents the prefix definitions.

Listing 3.27 – *The namespace prefix definitions necessary for interactivity scenarios*
```
xmlns:i="clr-namespace:System.Windows.Interactivity;assembly=System.Windows.Interactivity"
xmlns:ei="clr-namespace:Microsoft.Expression.Interactivity.Core;assembly=Microsoft.Expression.Interactions"
```

We can also execute command objects when events other than the Click event are triggered. One such example is shown in the XAML code from listing 3.28.

Listing 3.28 – *Invoking the command when other events occur*
```
<Rectangle Fill="Red" Width="100" Height="50">
    <i:Interaction.Triggers>
        <i:EventTrigger EventName="MouseLeftButtonDown">
            <i:InvokeCommandAction
                Command="{Binding SaveCommand}"/>
        </i:EventTrigger>
    </i:Interaction.Triggers>
</Rectangle>
```

The code uses the InvokeCommandAction trigger action to execute a command when the user presses the mouse over the rectangle. The InvokeCommandAction class is defined in the System.Windows.Interactivity.dll assembly, so make sure to add the reference and the namespace prefix definition before using it.

The PRISM framework also allows us to use command behaviors in order to execute commands when interacting with elements that do not expose ICommand properties. These command behaviors are exposed through attached properties. PRISM provides a command behavior for the click event but we can build our own by following the PRISM implementation.

The ButtonBaseClickCommandBehavior behavior subscribes to the attached element Click event and executes the specified command when the Click event is fired. The PRISM implementation can be seen in listing 3.29.

Listing 3.29 – *Click command behavior definition*
```
public class ButtonBaseClickCommandBehavior :
        CommandBehaviorBase<ButtonBase>
{
    public ButtonBaseClickCommandBehavior(
        ButtonBase clickableObject) : base(clickableObject)
    {
        if (clickableObject == null)
            throw new System.ArgumentNullException(
```

```
            "clickableObject");
        clickableObject.Click += OnClick;
    }
    private void OnClick(object sender, System.Windows.RoutedEventArgs e)
    {
        ExecuteCommand();
    }
}
```

The command and command argument can be attached to an instance of this class by using attached properties. The PRISM framework offers the Click class just for this purpose. The code below presents an example of using the PRISM command behaviors. We can also implement our own behaviors by following the PRISM code.

```
<Button Content="Save" prism:Click.Command="{Binding SaveCommand}"
        prism:Click.CommandParameter="1"/>
```

Data validation

Data validation in WPF and Silverlight can be done in various ways. The most common method is to implement the IDataErrorInfo and INotifyDataErrorInfo interfaces. These interfaces will be implemented on the domain objects we need to validate. The IDataErrorInfo interface provides basic validation and error notification support. The interface definition can be seen in listing 3.30.

The interface exposes an indexer and a property. The indexer can be used by model or view-model classes to return error messages specific to a particular property. Returning a null value or an empty string means that the property value is valid. The property allows us to set a global error message. It should be noted that this property is not called by the WPF or Silverlight data binding engines.

Listing 3.30 – *The IDataErrorInfo interface definition*
```
public interface IDataErrorInfo
{
    string Error { get; }
    string this[string columnName] { get; }
}
```

The INotifyDataErrorInfo interface is used to provide asynchronous data validation. This interface also supports multiple errors for a single property. The interface is only supported in Silverlight 4 or later. The interface is not available for WPF. The code shown in listing 3.31 presents the interface definition.

Listing 3.31 – *The INotifyDataErrorInfo interface definition*
```
public interface INotifyDataErrorInfo
{
    bool HasErrors { get; }
    event EventHandler<DataErrorsChangedEventArgs> ErrorsChanged;
    IEnumerable GetErrors(string propertyName);
}
```

The HasErrors property indicates whether the entity has validation errors. The GetErrors method returns the errors for a particular property. The ErrorsChanged event is triggered when the entity errors change. This can mean the entity has no more errors or that the errors for a property have changed.

By default the WPF or Silverlight data binding engines do not report any errors to the UI. In order for errors to be reported we need to set some binding properties. The XAML code shown in listing 3.32 presents the content for the CustomerView view.

Listing 3.32 – *Specifying that validation errors should be displayed in the UI*
```xml
<TextBlock Text="First Name"/>
<TextBox Text="{Binding FirstName, Mode=TwoWay,
        UpdateSourceTrigger=PropertyChanged,
        ValidatesOnNotifyDataErrors=True}" />
<TextBlock Text="Last Name"/>
<TextBox Text="{Binding LastName, Mode=TwoWay,
        UpdateSourceTrigger=PropertyChanged,
        ValidatesOnNotifyDataErrors=True}" />
<TextBlock Text="Email"/>
<TextBox Text="{Binding Email, Mode=TwoWay,
        UpdateSourceTrigger=PropertyChanged,
        ValidatesOnNotifyDataErrors=True}" />
```

The bindings in the 3 text boxes set the ValidatesOnNotifyDataErrors property to true. This tells the data binding engine to monitor the INotifyDataErrorInfo interface implementation and modify the UI in case of errors. Other properties we could set on the binding are ValidatesOnDataErrors and ValidatesOnExceptions. The first property tells the data binding engine to monitor the IDataErrorInfo implementation and present the errors to the UI. The second property tells the data binding engine to present errors when exceptions are thrown in the property setters.

As you probably noticed, our application will use the INotifyDataErrorInfo interface to provide data validation. Since we may have multiple domain objects that need to be validated, it is a good idea to implement this interface in a base type. Add the class definition presented in listing 3.33 to the ViewModels folder of the Silverlight project.

Listing 3.33 – *Implementing the INotifyDataErrorInfo interface*
```csharp
public class DomainObject:NotificationObject,
        INotifyDataErrorInfo
{
    private ErrorsContainer<string> errorsContainer;
    public DomainObject()
    {
        errorsContainer = new ErrorsContainer<string>(
          p => RaiseErrorsChanged(p));
    }
    public event EventHandler<DataErrorsChangedEventArgs>
        ErrorsChanged;
    public IEnumerable GetErrors(string propertyName)
    {
        return errorsContainer.GetErrors(propertyName);
```

```
    }
    public bool HasErrors
    {
        get { return errorsContainer.HasErrors; }
    }
    protected virtual void ValidateProperty(string name,
        object value) { }
    protected void RaiseErrorsChanged(string name)
    {
        if (ErrorsChanged != null)
            ErrorsChanged(this,
                new DataErrorsChangedEventArgs(name));
    }
    protected ErrorsContainer<string> ErrorsContainer
    {
        get { return errorsContainer; }
    }
}
```

This class will implement the INotifyDataErrorInfo interface. It will also derive from NotificationObject in order to provide change notification events.

The INotifyDataErrorInfo interface is a little harder to implement compared to IDataErrorInfo because we need to maintain a list of errors for every view-model or model property. In order to make the implementation a little easier, PRISM offers the ErrorsContainer class. This class can be used to manage the validation errors in the implementing class. The above code presents how the ErrorsContainer class is used. You can see that in the interface implementation we delegate all responsibilities to an ErrorsContainer instance.

The important method in this implementation is ValidateProperty method. This virtual method will be overridden in the derived classes in order to provide validation. Add the following change to the CustomerViewModel definition.

```
public class CustomerViewModel : DomainObject
```

The CustomerViewModel view-model now derives from DomainObject. This allows the class to provide validation in addition to change notifications. Add the ValidateProperty method override to this class, as shown in listing 3.34.

Listing 3.34 – *Validating the Customer entity*
```
protected override void ValidateProperty(string name,
        object value)
{
    if (name == "FirstName")
    {
        List<string> errors = new List<string>();
        ValidateName(value as string, errors);
        ErrorsContainer.SetErrors(name, errors);
    }
    else if (name == "LastName")
    {
```

```csharp
        List<string> errors = new List<string>();
        ValidateName(value as string, errors);
        ErrorsContainer.SetErrors(name, errors);
    }
    else if (name == "Email")
    {
        List<string> errors = new List<string>();
        ValidateEmail(value as string, errors);
        ErrorsContainer.SetErrors(name, errors);
    }
    else { base.ValidateProperty(name, value); }
}
```

For each property we generate a new error list and store it in the ErrorsContainer instance. Storing an empty list will clear the errors for that property. After this method is implemented, we can call it in every property setter we wish to validate. The code presented in listing 3.35 shows an example for the FirstName property. The other properties call the ValidateProperty method in a similar fashion.

Listing 3.35 – *Validating the FirstName property*
```csharp
public string FirstName
{
    get { return customer.FirstName; }
    set
    {
        if (customer.FirstName == value) return;
        ValidateProperty("FirstName", value);
        customer.FirstName = value;
        RaisePropertyChanged("FirstName");
    }
}
```

The last code we need to implement is the code for the ValidateName and ValidateEmail methods. We want to establish the following rules: the first and last names should not exceed 20 characters, the first and last names should not be empty and should not container numbers and the email should be valid. Add the definitions for the other 2 validation methods as shown in listing 3.36.

Listing 3.36 – *The other validation methods*
```csharp
private void ValidateName(string name, List<string> errors)
{
    if (string.IsNullOrEmpty(name))
        errors.Add("Field cannot be empty.");
    if (name.Length > 20)
        errors.Add("Field cannot exceed 20 characters.");
    Regex reg = new Regex("[0-9]");
    if (reg.IsMatch(name))
        errors.Add("Field cannot contain numbers.");
}
private void ValidateEmail(string mail, List<string> errors)
{
```

```
    Regex reg = new Regex(@"^([0-9a-zA-Z]([-\.\w]*[0-9a-zA-Z])*@([0-9a-zA-Z][-\w]*[0-9a-zA-Z]\.)+[a-zA-Z]{2,9})$");
    if (!reg.IsMatch(mail))
        errors.Add("Invalid value.");
}
```

Running the application at this point should notify the user if he or she enters incorrect data. This can be seen in figure 3.3.

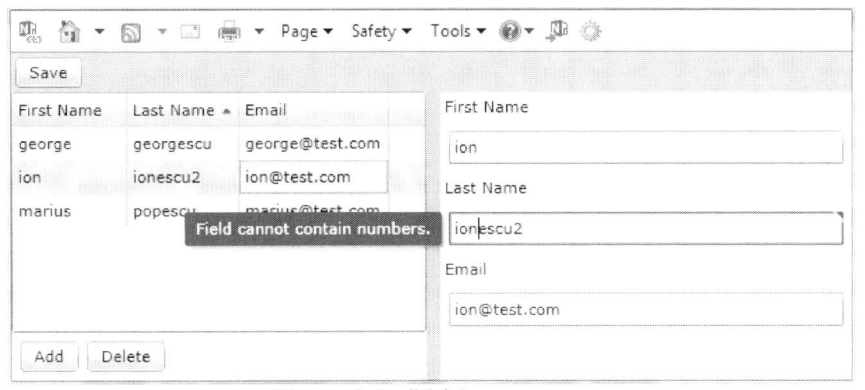

Figure 3.3 – *Validating user input*

The great thing about the INotifyDataErrorInfo interface is that you can use it to validate client data based on server side validation. One such example would be not allowing the user to add a new customer if the customer name exists in the database.

3.5 Summary

The Model-View-ViewModel pattern is a separation pattern. It allows developers and designers to work on the same application at the same time. The pattern does this by separating the application user interface logic from the business and presentation logic. This separation makes it easier for developers to test, maintain and extend the application.

This chapter described the MVVM components as well as the class interactions. The model represents the business logic and application data. The view represents the user interface. It is the part of the application that displays the data to the user. The view-model is the one that adapts the model so that it can be easily displayed in the view. The view-model implements a number of interfaces that enable change notification events and data validation. The view communicates with the view-model via commands. When commands are triggered in the view, the command handlers execute in the view-model in order to perform the required functionality.

CHAPTER 4: USER INTERACTION

Every application that offers a UI needs to interact with its users, either to display messages or to request confirmation before proceeding with a particular action. In a regular application this isn't a very difficult thing to do. All the developer has to do is invoke a MessageBox or display any other modal window in order to gather the required information.

Things get a little more difficult if this needs to be done in an MVVM application. We cannot display MessageBoxes or custom windows in a view-model because this will break the separation of concerns. Displaying MessageBoxes from a view-model will also make automated testing impossible. This is because, every time a test that accesses the MessageBox code is run, the user has to manually close the window for the test to continue.

There are a couple of solutions to this problem: interaction services and interaction request objects. The first option involves abstracting the message box interaction behind a service interface. The service instance is passed to the view-model via constructor injection and the code can then call the service methods every time a message box needs to be displayed. During testing the interaction service interface can be implemented to return dummy data. Interaction request objects trigger an event in the view model and a behavior in the XAML handles this event and displays the UI. When this UI is closed, the data is returned to the client view-model via a callback delegate. The sections that follow describe these 2 approaches to user interaction in more detail.

4.1 Using an interaction service

Create a new Silverlight project and add the code in listing 4.1 as the Application_Startup event handler in order to initialize the application.

Listing 4.1 – *Initializing the application*
```
private void Application_Startup(object sender, StartupEventArgs e)
{
    var view = new MainPage();
    var intService = new InteractionService();
    view.DataContext = new MainViewModel(intService);
    RootVisual = view;
}
```

This code instantiates the interaction service and injects it into the view-model constructor. A possible implementation for the interaction service is presented in listing 4.2.

Listing 4.2 – *The interaction service initial implementation*
```
public interface IInteractionService
{
    bool ShowConfirmation(string message, string caption);
}
public class InteractionService:IInteractionService
{
    public bool ShowConfirmation(string message, string caption)
    {
        var res = MessageBox.Show(message, caption,
          MessageBoxButton.OKCancel);
        if (res == MessageBoxResult.OK)
            return true;
        return false;
    }
}
```

Add the class definition presented in listing 4.3 to the project. The view-model exposes a command that is bound to a button in the UI. When this command is invoked the interaction service is used to display the confirmation message.

Listing 4.3 – *The application view model*
```
public class MainViewModel:NotificationObject
{
    private ObservableCollection<string> strings;
    public ObservableCollection<string> Strings
    {
        get { return strings; }
        set
        {
            if (strings == value) return;
            strings=value;
            RaisePropertyChanged("Strings");
        }
    }
    private DelegateCommand showCmd;
    private IInteractionService intService;
    public MainViewModel(IInteractionService intService)
    {
        this.intService = intService;
        showCmd = new DelegateCommand(OnShow);
    }
    public DelegateCommand ShowCommand { get { return showCmd; }}
    private void OnShow()
    {
        bool res = intService.ShowNotification("Are you sure?",
          "Delete Customer");
```

```
        if (res)
        {
            //...
        }
    }
}
```

This implementation forces a synchronous calling pattern that is only specific to WPF applications. Silverlight uses an asynchronous pattern. Implementing this service interface in Silverlight can be difficult when not using the MessageBox class.

A more appropriate implementation would be to specify a callback in the service interface. This callback can be called after the interaction with the user has finished. The callback interface is just as easy to implement in WPF as it is in Silverlight. Listing 4.4 presents the new interaction service implementation.

Listing 4.4 – *Interaction service using a callback delegate*
```
public interface IInteractionService
{
    void ShowConfirmation(string message, string caption,
        Action<bool> callback);
}
public class InteractionService:IInteractionService
{
    public void ShowConfirmation(string message, string caption,
        Action<bool> callback)
    {
        var res = MessageBox.Show(message, caption,
         MessageBoxButton.OKCancel);
        if (res == MessageBoxResult.OK)
        {
            callback(true); return;
        }
        callback(false);
    }
}
```

Modify the view-model code, as shown in listing 4.5, in order to use the new interaction service implementation.

Listing 4.5 – *Calling the new interaction service*
```
private void OnShow()
{
    intService.ShowNotification("Are you sure?",
        "Delete Customer", res => {
        if (!res) return;
        //...
    });
}
```

Using a MessageBox for user interaction is ok as long as the user is not required to provide any additional information. If the user needs to provide additional information or if the confirmation UI needs to be styled to fit the application theme, we can use a ChildWindow derived class. For WPF applications we can use Window derived classes to the same effect. A Silverlight implementation that uses a ChildWindow might look like the one in listing 4.6.

Listing 4.6 – *Interaction service that uses a ChildWindow derived class*
```
public class InteractionService:IInteractionService
{
    public void ShowConfirmation(string message, string caption,
        Action<bool> callback)
    {
        var wnd = new ConfirmationWindow();
        wnd.Title = caption;
        wnd.Message = message;
        EventHandler<CancelEventArgs> handler=null;
        handler = (s, e) => {
            wnd.Closing -= handler;
            if (wnd.DialogResult.HasValue &&
                wnd.DialogResult.Value)
                callback(true);
            else
                callback(false);
        };
        wnd.Closing += handler;
        wnd.Show();
    }
}
```

In the above listing, the ConfirmationWindow derives from ChildWindow. It adds the Title and Message properties and also 2 buttons that can be used to accept or cancel the operation. The code in listing 4.7 presents the XAML for the ConfirmationView.

Listing 4.7 – *The ConfirmationWindow XAML definition*
```
<Grid.RowDefinitions>
    <RowDefinition />
    <RowDefinition Height="Auto" />
</Grid.RowDefinitions>
<TextBlock Text="{Binding ElementName=wnd, Path=Message}"
        TextWrapping="Wrap"/>
<StackPanel Grid.Row="1" Orientation="Horizontal"
        HorizontalAlignment="Right" >
    <Button Content="OK" Click="OKButton_Click" Width="75"
        Margin="3"/>
    <Button Content="Cancel" Click="CancelButton_Click"
        Width="75" Margin="3"/>
</StackPanel>
```

As you can see, the TextBlock that displays the message is bound to the Message property defined in the code behind. The Click event handlers set the DialogResult property value in order to close the window. The code-behind for the ConfirmationWindow can be seen in listing 4.8.

Listing 4.8 – *The ConfirmationWindow code-behind*
```
public string Message { get; set; }
public string Title { get; set; }
private void OKButton_Click(object sender, RoutedEventArgs e)
{
    this.DialogResult = true;
}
private void CancelButton_Click(object sender, RoutedEventArgs e)
{
    this.DialogResult = false;
}
```

In the service implementation, we subscribe to the Closing event and then display the window. If, at closing time, the DialogResult property is true we pass true as the callback argument. Otherwise we call the callback with a false argument.

The current implementation is a little limiting. We could add more features in order to solve some additional problems and make the implementation more flexible.

In order to display multiple properties we could change the message type to something other than a string. To be able to also display simple notifications we will need to add a new method to the service interface and implement it. To make the service interface more flexible, and to allow the modified object to be used by the caller, we should encapsulate all interaction data in a single type. Given these considerations the new service interface definition will look like the one in listing 4.9.

Listing 4.9 – *Interaction service that uses an interaction object*
```
public class InteractionObject
{
    public string Title { get; set; }
    public object Content { get; set; }
    public bool Result { get; set; }
}

public interface IInteractionService
{
    void ShowConfirmation(InteractionObject message,
        Action<InteractionObject> callback);
    void ShowNotification(InteractionObject message,
        Action callback = null);
}
```

In the ConfirmationWindow code-behind remove the Title property and change the Message property type from string to InteractionObject as below.

```
public InteractionObject Message { get; set; }
```

In the ConfirmationWindow XAML use the following ContentControl to represent the content.

```
<ContentControl HorizontalContentAlignment="Stretch"
    VerticalContentAlignment="Stretch"
```

```
Content="{Binding Message.Content, ElementName=wnd}" />
```

Define a DataTemplate for each content type we want to use. In WPF and Silverlight 5 we can use the automatic data template feature, but in Silverlight 4 and earlier we have a problem. To support automatic data templates in earlier versions of Silverlight we need to build our own custom ContentControl that selects the appropriate DataTemplate from its Resources collection. PRISM supports such functionality through the DataTemplateSelector class.

The XAML in listing 4.10 presents the relevant portion of the new ConfirmationWindow UI. A DataTemplate for a custom type has also been added.

Listing 4.10 – *Main part of the ConfirmationWindow XAML definition*
```xml
<Grid.Resources>
    <DataTemplate DataType="loc:CustomMessage">
        <StackPanel>
            <TextBlock Text="{Binding FirstLine}"/>
            <TextBlock Text="{Binding SecondLine}"/>
        </StackPanel>
    </DataTemplate>
</Grid.Resources>
<Grid.RowDefinitions>
    <RowDefinition />
    <RowDefinition Height="Auto" />
</Grid.RowDefinitions>
<ContentControl HorizontalContentAlignment="Stretch"
        VerticalContentAlignment="Stretch"
        Content="{Binding Message.Content, ElementName=wnd}"/>
```

The new interaction service implementation can be seen in listing 4.11. This implementation also makes use of the new NotificationWindow child window. The NotificationWindow child window is implemented in a similar manner to the ConfirmationWindow class, but provides only an OK button.

Listing 4.11 – *The interaction service implementation using interaction objects*
```csharp
public class InteractionService:IInteractionService
{
    public void ShowConfirmation(InteractionObject message,
        Action<InteractionObject> callback)
    {
        var wnd = new ConfirmationWindow();
        wnd.Message = message;
        EventHandler<CancelEventArgs> handler = null;
        handler = (s, e) =>
        {
            wnd.Closing -= handler;
            if (wnd.DialogResult.HasValue &&
                    wnd.DialogResult.Value)
                callback(message);
            else
                callback(message);
        };
```

```
        wnd.Closing += handler;
        wnd.Show();
    }
    public void ShowNotification(InteractionObject message,
            Action callback=null)
    {
        var wnd = new NotificationWindow();
        wnd.Message = message;
        EventHandler<CancelEventArgs> handler = null;
        handler = (s, e) =>
        {
            wnd.Closing -= handler;
            if (callback != null) callback();
        };
        wnd.Closing += handler;
        wnd.Show();
    }
}
```

Listing 4.12 presents the view-model command handler with the modified code that uses the new version of the interaction service.

Listing 4.12 – *Using the new interaction service implementation*
```
private void OnShow()
{
    var obj = new InteractionObject()
    {
        Title = "Delete string",
        Content = "Are you sure?"
    };
    intService.ShowConfirmation(obj, callback =>
    {
        if (!callback.Result) return;
        strings.RemoveAt(0);
    });
}
```

There are still some changes that can be made to improve our implementation. Adding data templates to the confirmation and notification windows, to support all possible scenarios, decouples the template from the view where the interaction occurs. This can make it difficult to update and maintain the code since the user needs to look in multiple places to understand a single view. A better solution would be to supply the data template in the view where the interaction occurs. This is also useful if we need to display the same data type in multiple ways. Another change we might like to make is to check for data validity and only allow the OK button to be pressed if the data is valid. All these shortcomings are addressed by interaction request objects.

4.1.1 Testing with the interaction service
In order to add a unit test project to test Silverlight assemblies we need to install the Silverlight

toolkit. The toolkit installs the Silverlight unit testing assemblies. A Silverlight test project is just a normal Silverlight application project that has references to the Silverlight unit testing assemblies: Microsoft.VisualStudio.QualityTools.UnitTesting.Silverlight.dll and Microsoft.Silverlight.Testing.dll.

Create a new Silverlight project and choose not to host it anywhere. Add references to the assemblies specified earlier and also delete the MainPage file since the application UI will be generated automatically. Also set the project as the startup project. Modify the Application_Startup event handler like in listing 4.13 in order to create the root visual.

Listing 4.13 – *Creating the test page and setting it as the root visual element*
```
private void Application_Startup(object sender,
        StartupEventArgs e)
{
    this.RootVisual = UnitTestSystem.CreateTestPage();
}
```

At this point the test application is ready to be run. Figure 4.1 presents the user interface for the test project.

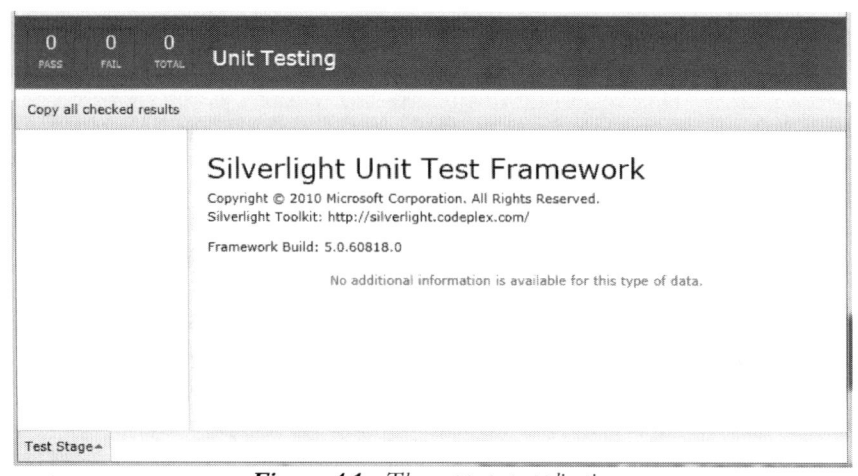

Figure 4.1 – *The empty test application*

The upper parts of the interface shows an overview of the testing process. It shows how many tests passed or failed. It also shows the total number of tests run. The left pane shows a hierarchical view of the tests. Each test will be grouped by the class that contains it. When a test is selected, the main area of the interface will present the test details.

Before we can test the view-model we need to create a mock of the interaction service. Add the class definition shown in listing 4.14 to the test project.

Listing 4.14 – *Mocking the interaction service*
```
public class MockInteractionService:IInteractionService
{
    public bool ReturnTrue { get; set; }
    public void ShowConfirmation(InteractionObject message,
```

```
            Action<InteractionObject> callback)
    {
        message.Result = ReturnTrue;
        if (callback != null) callback(message);
    }
    public void ShowNotification(InteractionObject message,
            Action callback = null)
    {
        if (callback != null) callback();
    }
}
```

In order to create this class definition we need to add a reference to the project that defines the service interface. This implementation uses a boolean property that determines the value returned by the confirmation callback.

Add the test class shown in listing 4.15 to the test project in order to test the confirmation operation.

Listing 4.15 *– Testing the confirmation*
```
[TestClass]
public class UnitTests
{
    [TestMethod]
    public void ConfirmingDeletesStrings()
    {
        var intService = new MockInteractionService()
          { ReturnTrue = true };
        var vm = new MainViewModel(intService);
        vm.Strings = new ObservableCollection<string>();
        vm.Strings.Add("demo");
        vm.OnShow();
        Assert.AreEqual(0, vm.Strings.Count);
    }
}
```

Running the test application presents an interface similar to the one presented in figure 4.2. You can see that the test passed. Similar tests can be written to test what happens if the user cancels the request.

4.2 Using interaction request objects

Another option for user interaction is to use interaction request objects. These objects expose an event that is triggered every time a view-model needs to initiate an interaction. The UI decides how this interaction will take place by subscribing to the event, via a behavior, and displaying some kind of window. This is the approach to interaction that PRISM takes. Interaction request objects are represented in PRISM by the IInteractionRequest interface. The definition can be seen in listing 4.16.

Listing 4.16 *– The IInteractionRequest interface definition*
```
public interface IInteractionRequest
{
```

```
    event EventHandler<InteractionRequestedEventArgs> Raised;
}
```

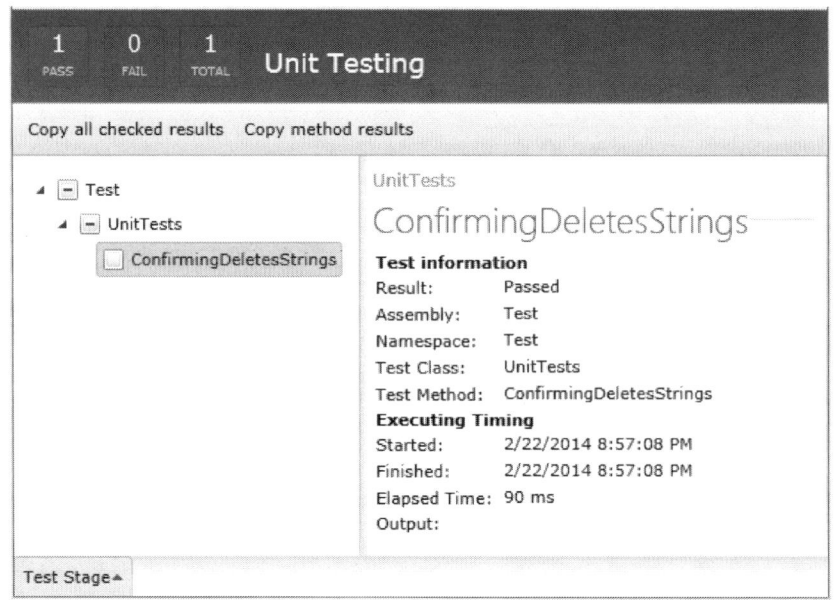

Figure 4.2 – *The test application containing a single test*

PRISM offers a single implementation of the IInteractionRequest interface in the form of the InteractionRequest<T> class. This implementation exposes a method named Raise that raises the Raised event. There are 2 overloads of the Raise method. One overload requires a callback that will be invoked when the interaction is over. This callback will allow the user to interact with the data that has been modified as a result of the interaction. This method definition is presented in listing 4.17.

Listing 4.17 – *Invoking the Raised event in InteractionRequest<T>*
```
public void Raise(T context, Action<T> callback)
{
    var handler = this.Raised;
    if (handler != null)
    {
        handler(this, new InteractionRequestedEventArgs(
          context, () => callback(context)));
    }
}
```

The generic type argument is an instance of the Notification class. This type exposes 2 properties: Title of type string and Content of type object. PRISM also offers a class that is used for confirmation scenarios. This functionality is implemented by the Confirmation class. This class derives from the Notification class and adds a Confirm property of type bool.

On the view-model side we will create an IInteractionRequest<T> instance and use it to request the interaction by calling the Raise method. On the view side, the view will subscribe to this event via an EventTrigger and will display some sort of popup window. PRISM offers such event triggers and popups only for Silverlight. If we want to use this interaction pattern in WPF we would have to implement our own trigger action in order to display some kind of window and interact with the user. The sections that follow present an example of using the interaction request object pattern.

Creating the application
For this example we will create a Silverlight application with 2 buttons. Clicking one button will display a notification. Clicking the second button will display a confirmation dialog. After the Silverlight project is created we need to add references to the following assemblies from the PRISM installation path: Microsoft.Expression.Interactions.dll, Microsoft.Practices.Prism.Interactivity.dll, Microsoft.Practices.Prism.dll and System.Windows.Interactivity.dll,.

Add the definition presented in listing 4.18 as the Application_Startup event handler in order to initialize the application.

Listing 4.18 – *Initializing the application*
```
private void Application_Startup(object sender,
        StartupEventArgs e)
{
    var view = new MainPage();
    view.DataContext = new MainViewModel();
    App.Current.RootVisual = view;
}
```

The MainViewModel view-model class will expose our 2 interaction request objects. Add the class definition presented in listing 4.19 to the Silverlight project.

Listing 4.19 – *Defining the application view-model*
```
public class MainViewModel
{
    private readonly InteractionRequest<Notification> msgReq;
    private readonly InteractionRequest<Confirmation> confReq;
    public MainViewModel()
    {
        msgReq = new InteractionRequest<Notification>();
        confReq = new InteractionRequest<Confirmation>();
    }

    public IInteractionRequest MessageRequest
    {
        get { return msgReq; }
    }
    public IInteractionRequest ConfirmationRequest
    {
        get { return confReq; }
    }
}
```

Using the IInteractionRequest objects
The view-model currently exposes the two IInteractionRequest instances. The view will subscribe to

the Raised events defined by these instances in order to present the interaction views. Add the commands shown in listing 4.20 to the view-model.

Listing 4.20 – *Defining the commands that will invoke the interaction request objects*
```
private DelegateCommand msgCmd, confCmd;
public DelegateCommand MessageCommand
{
    get
    {
        if (msgCmd == null)
            msgCmd = new DelegateCommand(OnMessage);
        return msgCmd;
    }
}
public DelegateCommand ConfirmCommand
{
    get
    {
        if (confCmd == null)
            confCmd = new DelegateCommand(OnConfirm);
        return confCmd;
    }
}
```

These 2 commands will be bound to 2 buttons in the view. When these buttons are pressed, their handlers will call the Raise method of each interaction request object. Add the handlers shown in listing 4.21 to the view-model class.

Listing 4.21 – *Implementing the command handlers*
```
private void OnMessage()
{
    var n = new Notification() { Title = "title",
        Content = "content" };
    msgReq.Raise(n);
}
private void OnConfirm()
{
    var c = new Confirmation() { Title = "title", Content = "content" };
    confReq.Raise(c, res => {
        if (!res.Confirmed) return;
        //do something
    });
}
```

Constructing the view
Add 2 buttons to the view and bind them to the commands exposed from the view model as shown in listing 4.22.

Listing 4.22 – *Binding the view-model commands*
```
<Button Content="Message" Command="{Binding MessageCommand}"
```

```
            Grid.Column="0"/>
<Button Content="Confirm" Command="{Binding ConfirmCommand}"
    Grid.Column="1"/>
```

Add the following namespace prefixes to the view.

```
xmlns:prism="http://www.codeplex.com/prism"
xmlns:i="clr-
namespace:System.Windows.Interactivity;assembly=System.Windows.Interactivity"
```

Add the triggers presented in listing 4.23 to the view. These triggers will subscribe to the Raised event exposed by the interaction request objects. The InteractionRequestTrigger class derives from EventTrigger and overrides the GetEventName method in order to always return the Raised event. We could have used a regular EventTrigger and supplied Raised for the EventName attribute as well.

Listing 4.23 – *Defining the triggers that will display the interaction windows*
```
<UserControl.Resources>
    <DataTemplate x:Key="template">
        <TextBlock Text="{Binding}" />
    </DataTemplate>
</UserControl.Resources>
<i:Interaction.Triggers>
    <prism:InteractionRequestTrigger SourceObject="{Binding MessageRequest}">
        <prism:PopupChildWindowAction ContentTemplate="{StaticResource template}" />
    </prism:InteractionRequestTrigger>
    <prism:InteractionRequestTrigger SourceObject="{Binding ConfirmationRequest}">
        <prism:PopupChildWindowAction
          ContentTemplate="{StaticResource template}" />
    </prism:InteractionRequestTrigger>
</i:Interaction.Triggers>
```

PopupChildWindowAction
Running the application at this point should allow you to press the buttons and view the notification and confirmation windows. All this is made possible by the PopupChildWindowAction class.

The PopupChildWindowAction class derives from PopupChildWindowActionBase and adds 2 properties: ContentTemplate and ChildWindow. The ContentTemplate property defines the DataTemplate that will be used when displaying the Notification.Content property. The ChildWindow property defines a new ChildWindow that will be used in the interaction. You can define your own child window to provide data validation for example.

The class also overrides the base GetChildWindow method. This method determines the window that gets displayed when the Raised event is fired. The method definition can be seen in listing 4.24.

Listing 4.24 – *The GetChildWindow method definition*
```
protected override ChildWindow GetChildWindow(
        Notification notification)
{
    var childWindow = this.ChildWindow ??
```

```
        this.CreateDefaultWindow(notification);
    childWindow.DataContext = notification;
    return childWindow;
}

private ChildWindow CreateDefaultWindow(
        Notification notification)
{
    return notification is Confirmation ?
(ChildWindow)new ConfirmationChildWindow {
ConfirmationTemplate = this.ContentTemplate } : new NotificationChildWindow {
        NotificationTemplate = this.ContentTemplate };
}
```

You can see that a different window is returned depending on the notification type. Also we have the option of specifying our own window class if the provided ones don't suit our needs. The main work is done in the base class' Invoke method. PopupChildWindowActionBase is a TriggerAction. Its Invoke method has the definition presented in listing 4.25.

Listing 4.25 – *Displaying the interaction window*
```
protected override void Invoke(object parameter)
{
    var args = parameter as InteractionRequestedEventArgs;
    if (args == null) return;
    var childWindow = this.GetChildWindow(args.Context);
    var callback = args.Callback;
    EventHandler handler = null;
    handler = (o, e) => {
        childWindow.Closed -= handler;
        callback();
    };
    childWindow.Closed += handler;
    childWindow.Show();
}
```

You can see that this implementation is very similar to what we did while implementing the InteractionService. The code instantiates a new ChildWindow depending on the notification type. After this, an EventHandler is created and attached to the child window closed event. After the window is closed the code calls the callback delegate.

Interaction requests in WPF

The TriggerAction and child windows presented previously, are implemented only in the Silverlight version of PRISM. Using the Silverlight implementation as an example we can easily build a WPF equivalent. Create a new WPF project and remove the StartupUri attribute from the App.xaml file. Add the override for the OnStartup method, presented in listing 4.26, in order to initialize the application.

Listing 4.26 – *Initializing the WPF application*
```
protected override void OnStartup(StartupEventArgs e)
```

```
{
    base.OnStartup(e);
    var vm = new MainViewModel();
    var view = new MainWindow();
    view.DataContext = vm;
    App.Current.MainWindow = view;
    view.Show();
}
```

Add the class definition presented in listing 4.27 in order to define the view-model that will expose the interaction request.

Listing 4.27 – *The application view-model*
```
public class MainViewModel:NotificationObject
{
    private readonly InteractionRequest<Confirmation> confReq;
    private readonly DelegateCommand okCmd;
    public MainViewModel()
    {
        confReq = new InteractionRequest<Confirmation>();
        okCmd = new DelegateCommand(OnOk);
    }
    public IInteractionRequest ConfirmationRequest
    { get { return confReq; } }
    public ICommand OkCommand { get { return okCmd; } }
    public void OnOk()
    {
        var conf = new Confirmation() { Title = "Title",
         Content = "Are you sure?" };
        confReq.Raise(conf, c => {
            if (!c.Confirmed) return;
            //...
        });
    }
}
```

This view-model also exposes a command that will be bound to a button in the view. When the button is pressed the command handler is executed and the Raised event is triggered. This will allow the view to display the interaction window.

In order to implement the trigger action we also need to import the following assemblies: System.Windows.Interactivity.dll and Microsoft.Expression.Interactions.dll. These are located in the PRISM installation folder under the Lib directory. Add the class definition shown in listing 4.28 in order to define the trigger action.

Listing 4.28 – *Defining the custom trigger action*
```
public class InteractionActionBase:
         TriggerAction<FrameworkElement>
{
    protected override void Invoke(object parameter) { }
    protected abstract UserControl GetContent(
```

```
            Notification notification);
}
```

The implementation provides an additional abstract method named GetContent. This method will be used to retrieve the user control that will be displayed in order to interact with the user. We are returning a user control instead of a window because we might have to show the interaction UI multiple times. Once a window is closed it cannot be used anymore. This method will be implemented in a derived class.

Add the code presented in listing 4.29 at the beginning of the Invoke method in order to create the interaction window.

Listing 4.29 – *Creating the interaction window*
```
var args = parameter as InteractionRequestedEventArgs;
if (args == null) return;
var content = this.GetContent(args.Context);
var wnd = new Window();
wnd.WindowStartupLocation = WindowStartupLocation.CenterOwner;
wnd.Owner = Application.Current.MainWindow;
wnd.Title = args.Context.Title;
wnd.Content = content;
```

This code first returns the content to be displayed based on the notification type. After this it creates the window and sets its title and content. Every time the Invoke method is called a new window is created. After this, the window needs to be displayed. Add the code presented in listing 4.30 at the end of the Invoke method in order to display the window.

Listing 4.30 – *Hooking up the action delegates and showing the interaction window*
```
if (content is IConfirmationContent)
{
    IConfirmationContent cc = (IConfirmationContent)content;
    cc.OkAction += () => { wnd.Close(); };
    cc.CancelAction += () => { wnd.Close(); };
}
else if (content is INotificationContent)
{
    INotificationContent nc = (INotificationContent)content;
    nc.OkAction += () => { wnd.Close(); };
}
var callback = args.Callback;
EventHandler handler = null;
handler = (s, e) => {
    wnd.Closed -= handler;
    callback();
};
wnd.Closed += handler;
wnd.ShowDialog();
```

The first part of the code checks the notification type. Based on the notification type the code assigns methods to the OkAction and CancelAction delegates. These delegates will be called by the user control code when the user presses the OK and Cancel buttons respectively. They signal that the interaction window needs to be closed.

In order to make this solution more extensible, we expose these delegates by using two interfaces. By implementing these interfaces when we define a new user control, we can specify when the containing window should close without modifying the TriggerAction code. This is especialy useful if we implement this code in its own assembly in order to maximize the reuse possibilities. Listing 4.31 shows the interface implementations.

Listing 4.31 – *The notification interface definitions*
```
public interface INotificationContent
{
    Action OkAction { get; set; }
}
public interface IConfirmation:INotificationContent
{
    Action CancelAction { get; set; }
}
```

At the end of the Invoke method we create a handler that handles the Window.Close event. When this event is triggered we invoke our callback method so that the user can retrieve the modified content.

To finish the TriggerAction implementation we need to add a derived class that implements the GetContent method. Add the class definition shown in listing 4.32 to define this class.

Listing 4.32 – *Providing the content and content template properties*
```
public class InteractionAction:InteractionActionBase
{
    public static readonly DependencyProperty
        CustomConentProperty = DependencyProperty.Register(
        "CustomContent", typeof(UserControl),
        typeof(InteractionAction), new PropertyMetadata(null));
    public static readonly DependencyProperty
        ContentTemplateProperty = DependencyProperty.Register(
        "ContentTemplate", typeof(DataTemplate),
        typeof(InteractionAction), new PropertyMetadata(null));

    public UserControl CustomContent
    {
        get { return (UserControl) GetValue(CustomConentProperty); }
        set { SetValue(CustomConentProperty, value); }
    }
    public DataTemplate ContentTemplate
    {
        get { return (DataTemplate) GetValue(ContentTemplateProperty); }
        set { SetValue(ContentTemplateProperty, value); }
    }
}
```

This class adds two dependency properties in order to define the ContentTemplate and the

CustomContent (in case we want to display other content than the one provided by the default implementation). Add the implementation for the GetConent abstract method as shown in listing 4.33.

Listing 4.33 – *Getting the content based on the notification type*
```
protected override UserControl GetContent( Notification notification)
{
    UserControl content = CustomContent?? CreateDefaultContent(notification);
    content.DataContext = notification;
    return content;
}
private UserControl CreateDefaultContent( Notification notification)
{
    if (notification is Confirmation)
      return new ConfirmationContent {
         ConfirmationTemplate = this.ContentTemplate };
    return new NotificationContent {
         NotificationTemplate = this.ContentTemplate };
}
```

This code returns the custom content if it is set, otherwise it returns the default content based on the notification type. The only thing left to do is to implement the user controls that get returned from the CreateDefaultContent method. Add a new user control to the project and name it NotificationContent. Listing 4.34 presents the user control's code-behind. You can see that the user control also implements the INotificationContent interface in order to expose the OkAction action.

Listing 4.34 – *The NotificationContent code-behind contents.*
```
public partial class NotificationContent : UserControl, INotificationContent
{
    public NotificationContent()
    {
        InitializeComponent();
    }
    public Action OkAction { get; set; }
    public static readonly DependencyProperty NotificationTemplateProperty =
        DependencyProperty.Register("NotificationTemplate",
        typeof(DataTemplate), typeof(NotificationContent),
        new PropertyMetadata(null));
    public DataTemplate NotificationTemplate
    {
        get { return (DataTemplate)GetValue(NotificationTemplateProperty); }
        set { SetValue(NotificationTemplateProperty, value); }
    }
    private void btnOk_Click(object sender, RoutedEventArgs e)
    {
        if (OkAction != null) OkAction();
    }
}
```

The XAML for this user control can be seen in listing 4.35. Here, wnd is the name of the user control. The binding uses it to access the NotificationTemplate property defined in the code-behind.

Listing 4.35 – *The NotificationContent XAML definition*
```xml
<Grid.RowDefinitions>
    <RowDefinition Height="*"/>
    <RowDefinition Height="auto"/>
</Grid.RowDefinitions>
<ContentControl Content="{Binding Content}" ContentTemplate=
        "{Binding NotificationTemplate, ElementName=wnd}"
    HorizontalAlignment="Stretch" VerticalAlignment="Stretch"/>
<StackPanel Grid.Row="1" HorizontalAlignment="Right">
    <Button Content="Ok" Margin="2" Padding="5,2"
        Width="70" Click="btnOk_Click"/>
</StackPanel>
```

The code for the ConfirmationContent user control can be defined in the same way. The exception is that we also have a cancel button and in the OK button event handler we retrieve the Confirmation instance and set the Confirmed property to true. This can be seen in the listing 4.36.

Listing 4.36 – *Setting the Confirmed property in the ConfirmationWindow code-behind*
```csharp
private void btnOk_Click(object sender, RoutedEventArgs e)
{
    Confirmation c = DataContext as Confirmation;
    if (c != null) c.Confirmed = true;
    if (OkAction != null) OkAction();
}
private void btnCancel_Click(object sender, RoutedEventArgs e)
{
    if (CancelAction != null) CancelAction();
}
```

Make sure you also implement the IConfirmationContent interface in order to expose the OkAction and CancelAction actions.

4.2.1 Testing with interaction request objects

To test the WPF interaction request we need to add a new test project to our solution. We also need to add a reference to the main application so that we can test the view-model. Right click on the solution and choose Add New Project. Add a new Unit Test Project and after the project is created, add a reference to the assembly that contains your view-model.

Before writing the test we need to add a collection to the view-model that is modified when the command is invoked. Add the code presented in listing 4.37 to the MainViewModel class.

Listing 4.37 – *Adding a string collection to the view-model*
```csharp
private ObservableCollection<string> strings;
public ObservableCollection<string> Strings
{
    get { return strings; }
    set
    {
```

```
        if (strings == value) return;
        strings = value;
        RaisePropertyChanged("Strings");
    }
}
```

The Ok command handler has needs to be modified in order to actually delete something. This can be seen in listing 4.38.

Listing 4.38 – *Deleting a string if the operation is confirmed*
```
public void OnOk()
{
    var conf = new Confirmation()
    { Title = "Delete String", Content = "Are you sure?" };
    confReq.Raise(conf, c =>
    {
        if (!c.Confirmed) return;
        if (Strings.Count > 0) Strings.RemoveAt(0);
    });
}
```

We are now ready to write our first test. Add the test method presented in listing 4.39 to the test class.

Listing 4.39 – *Testing the interaction request object usage*
```
[TestMethod]
public void AcceptDeleteRequest_DeletesString()
{
    MainViewModel vm = new MainViewModel();
    vm.Strings = new ObservableCollection<string>();
    vm.Strings.Add("demo");
    vm.ConfirmationRequest.Raised += (s, e) => {
        Confirmation c = e.Context as Confirmation;
        if (c == null) return;
        c.Confirmed = true;
        e.Callback();
    };
    vm.OnOk();
    Assert.AreEqual(0, vm.Strings.Count);
}
```

Running the test should have the effect of removing the string. All this without having to interact with the application in any way. A similar test can be added that cancels the interaction.

4.3 Summary

This chapter talked about user interaction. Almost any application interacts with the user by displaying messages or requiring input. Showing message boxes is easy enough, but this cannot be done is we are using UI separation patterns in order to make our application easier to extend, test and maintain. Displaying message boxes in view-models will affect automated testing since the developer will need to manually close the windows in order for the tests to continue. There are a couple of solutions to this problem and all of them abstract the process of displaying a UI.

Interaction services abstract the process of displaying an interaction window behind a service. The service implementation will provide and display the window as it sees fit. During testing we can then replace that implementation with a dummy implementation that returns hardcoded values. Using this mock service implementation will allow the tests to run without human intervention.

PRISM uses interaction request objects to display the interaction views. The interaction object exposes an event that will be triggered in the view-model every time an interaction is required. In the view, a trigger will subscribe to the interaction request event. When the event is raised the trigger action associated with the trigger will display the interaction view. When the view closes, the modified data is passed back to the view model via a callback delegate.Insert chapter four text here.

CHAPTER 5: INTER-MODULE COMMUNICATIONS

Even if composite applications have loosely coupled modules, developed independently of each other, these modules should still communicate in order to achieve the application functionality. There are multiple ways for modules to communicate with each other in a loosely coupled fashion. This chapter will talk about the following 3 options: commands, events and shared services.

PRISM composite commands can contain a list of ICommand implementations that get executed every time the composite command is executed. View-models in each module can register their local commands to globally available composite commands in order to execute local module code when another module (or the Shell) triggers the command.

The IEventAggregator service provides a means for consumers to publish or subscribe to loosely coupled events. Regular events require the subscriber to have a hard reference to the publisher. PRISM decouples the publisher from the subscriber allowing the event to be the center of the interaction. A module can publish an event and anyone can subscribe to it without having a hard reference to the module that published it.

Shared services are services that can be accessed through a public interface by different modules. The interface is defined in a shared assembly while the service implementation is local to the defining module or Shell. The implementation is not shared. The service is accessed by using the DI container.

The following sections will describe these 3 options by building a simple document editing application.

5.1 Composite Commands

The CompositeCommand class is an ICommand implementation offered by PRISM that allows for command based communication between loosely coupled modules. This is possible because a CompositeCommand instance can hold references to commands defined in the same or other modules. ICommand instances can be registered with the CompositeCommand as shown in listing 5.1.

Listing 5.1 – *Registering commands with a CompositeCommand*
```
var saveCmd=new DelegateCommand(OnSave, CanSave);
```

`SaveAllCommand.RegisterCommand(saveCmd);`

When the view-model is not needed anymore the commands can be unregistered as shown below.

`SaveAllCommand.UnregisterCommand(saveCmd);`

Possible scenarios for using a CompositeCommand include: save and save all commands in the shell toolbar that save opened documents, Zoom-in and Zoom-out commands in the shell toolbar that can scale content in the current document and any scenario where a module (or the Shell) offers a command that needs to be handled in another module. Another example might include a shutdown command that needs to have all documents saved before closing the application.

To allow for the save and zoom scenarios, the CompositeCommand class executes only the active commands and also determines its execution status based on the active commands' execution status.

Any implementation of the ICommand interface can be registered with a CompositeCommand instance but usually we will register DelegateCommand instances. This is convenient also because the DelegateCommand class implements the IActiveAware interface. This allows a command to specify whether it is active in a particular context. If, for example, a CompositeCommand has a collection of DelegateCommands that have been registered, and command activity is monitored, when invoking the CompositeCommand only the active DelegateCommand instances will be executed. This is perfect for implementing the save and zoom scenarios from above, where only the current document needs to be taken into consideration when the toolbar commands are triggered. A CompositeCommand can monitor command activity by using the appropriate constructor, as shown below.

`public static readonly CompositeCommand SaveCommand = new CompositeCommand(true);`

To demonstrate the use of the CompositeCommand class in communicating across modules we will build a simple text editing application. The application will be written in WPF and will have a single module. The module will contain the text editing feature. At first there will be a few hardcoded documents that will be editable but this will change as the application evolves.

Since the CompositeCommands displayed in the Shell will need to be accessed from multiple parts in the application these commands will need to be defined in a common assembly. The following sections will describe the steps required to build and run the application.

Creating the project structure

Open VisualStudio and create an empty solution. The initial solution structure will contain the following assemblies: the Shell assembly which is a WPF application, the Infrastructure assembly and the EditingModule assembly. These last two assemblies are WPF user control libraries.

Before we do anything else, we need to add references to the PRISM assemblies from our Shell project. We will be using Unity, so make sure you add the Unity specific assemblies. These references can be added from the PRISM install path or you can copy them to another location closer to the project and reference them from the new location. This is actually a better solution in case you want to check-in your code to TFS. For the Infrastructure assembly just add a reference to the

Microfost.Practices.Prism.dll assembly. For the EditingModule module assembly add references to: Microsoft.Practices.Prism.dll and Microsoft.Practices.Unity.dll assemblies.

We also need to add references to the Infrastructure assembly from the Shell and EditingModule assemblies. The Infrastructure project will contain all the shared application logic. This can include: global commands, events, shared service interfaces and other shared types that need to be accessed by the entire application. In a PRISM application each module will usually have a reference to an assembly that will contain common application code. The project structure should look like the one presented in figure 5.1.

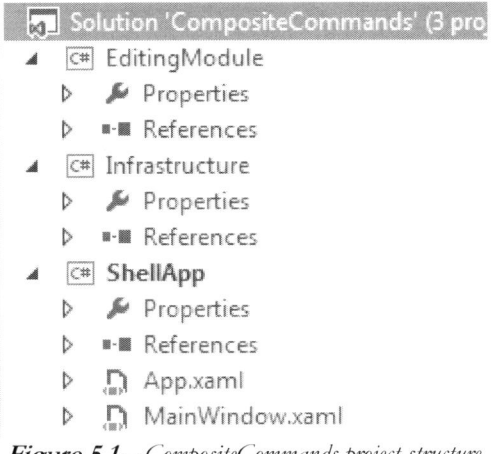

Figure 5.1 – *CompositeCommands project structure*

Creating the CompositeCommand instances

The Infrastructure project will contain the definitions for the composite commands. In order for these to be accessible from everywhere in the application we will define them in a static class. Add the class definition presented in listing 5.2 to the Infrastructure project.

Listing 5.2 – *Defining the global application commands*
```
public static class GlobalCommands
{
    public static readonly CompositeCommand SaveAllCommand =
        new CompositeCommand();
    public static readonly CompositeCommand SaveCommand =
        new CompositeCommand(true);
    public static readonly CompositeCommand ZoomInCommand =
        new CompositeCommand(true);
    public static readonly CompositeCommand ZoomOutCommand =
        new CompositeCommand(true);
}
```

Only the SaveAllCommand command will not monitor command activity. This is because this command needs to operate on all opened documents, not just the current one. Since the rest of the commands need to operate only on the current document they use the constructor that allows them to monitor command activity.

Initializing the Application

The application initialization is done using a custom UnityBootstrapper class. In the Shell project, create a new Bootstrapper class as shown in listing 5.3.

Listing 5.3 – *The application bootstrapper definition*
```
public class Bootstrapper:UnityBootstrapper
{
    protected override DependencyObject CreateShell()
    {
        return new MainWindow();
    }
    protected override void InitializeShell()
    {
        var view = (MainWindow)this.Shell;
        App.Current.MainWindow = view;
        App.Current.MainWindow.Show();
    }
}
```

The bootstrapper overrides the methods that create and initialize the Shell view. Be careful here to call the Show method. Calling ShowDialog will block the thread and the application modules will not load. An instance of this bootstrapper will need to be created and run in the OnStartup method override in order to initialize the application. This can be seen in listing 5.4. Make sure you remove the StartupUri property from the App.xaml file.

Listing 5.4 – *The application startup code*
```
protected override void OnStartup(StartupEventArgs e)
{
    base.OnStartup(e);
    new Bootstrapper().Run();
}
```

Defining the Shell

The Shell has a very simple structure. It exposes a toolbar with the 4 commands and a tab control that will represent the main region of the application. This main region will be used to display the documents. The XAML in listing 5.5 presents the toolbar.

Listing 5.5 – *The application toolbar*
```
<ToolBar Grid.Row="0">

<Button Content="Save All" Command="{x:Static inf:GlobalCommands.SaveAllCommand}" />
    <Button Content="Save" Command="{x:Static inf:GlobalCommands.SaveCommand}" />
    <Button Content="Zoom In" Command="{x:Static inf:GlobalCommands.ZoomInCommand}" />
    <Button Content="Zoom Out" Command="{x:Static inf:GlobalCommands.ZoomOutCommand}"/>
</ToolBar>
```

We also need to add the Infrastructure namespace prefix to the XAML file in order to use the

CompositeCommands. Specifying the commands like this works very well in WPF applications but not so well in Silverlight applications. There is no x:Static markup extension in Silverlight. One possible way to fix this problem is to expose the static commands as properties in the Shell view-model and data-bind to those properties instead. This can be done like in listing 5.6.

Listing 5.6 – *Exposing the SaveAll command*
```
public ICommand SaveAllCommand
{
    get { return GlobalCommands.SaveAllCommand; }
}
```

The XAML below presents the tab control that will represent the application main region. I will talk about regions in more detail in other chapters. I will talk a little about them here, as well, in order to understand the big picture about why we are using them in this example.

PRISM regions are named placeholders that allow us to decouple the views from their locations inside the Shell. This way, different modules can contribute views to the application, in a loosely coupled manner, and not have to worry about where they will be placed. This is achieved by using the IRegionManager service. PRISM regions can contain 0 or more views and these views can be added to a region in multiple ways: view discovery, view injection and view navigation. Since our editing view is defined in a separate module and we want to add multiple instances of this view to the Shell application, we will have to define the region that will contain our views. The views will then be added via view injection by using the IRegion.Add method. Listing 5.7 presents the main region XAML definition

Listing 5.7 – *The MainRegion XAML definition*
```xml
<TabControl Grid.Row="1" prism:RegionManager.RegionName="MainRegion">
   <TabControl.ItemContainerStyle>
      <Style TargetType="{x:Type TabItem}">
        <Setter Property="Header" Value="{Binding DataContext}"/>
        <Setter Property="HeaderTemplate">
           <Setter.Value>
              <DataTemplate>
                 <StackPanel Orientation="Horizontal">
                    <TextBlock Text="{Binding Title,
                        Converter={StaticResource tConv}}" />
                    <TextBlock Text="{Binding IsDirty,
                        Converter={StaticResource dConv}}"/>
                 </StackPanel>
              </DataTemplate>
           </Setter.Value>
        </Setter>
      </Style>
   </TabControl.ItemContainerStyle>
</TabControl>
```

Make sure you add the PRISM namespace prefix to the Shell xaml file. Regions can be defined in XAML by using the RegionManager.RegionName attached property. The XAML also presents the style that is applied to every TabItem instance. The style is used to set the header content.

We are also using 2 value converters here: one to display the dirty state of the document and the other to display the document title as just the file name. Both value converters are added as static resources to the Shell's ResourceDictionary collection. The relevant part of the DirtyStarConverter value converter can be seen in the listing 5.8.

Listing 5.8 – *The dirty value converter*
```
public class DirtyStarConverter:IValueConverter
{
    public object Convert(object value, Type targetType, object parameter,
            CultureInfo culture)
    {
        if (value is bool && (bool)value)
            return "*";
        return "";
    }
    //...
}
```

The relevant part of the TitleConverter can be seen in listing 5.9. You can see here that if the Document title is null the converter displays some default text. Otherwise it displays just the file name.

Listing 5.9 – *The TitleConverter converter definition*
```
public class TitleConverter:IValueConverter
{
    public object Convert(object value, Type targetType, object parameter,
            CultureInfo culture)
    {
        string str = value as string;
        if (string.IsNullOrEmpty(str)) return "(Untitled)";
        return Path.GetFileName(str);
    }
    //...
}
```

Now that the converters have been defined, make sure you add them as static resources so that they can be correctly referenced in the header template. This can be seen in listing 5.10.

Listing 5.10 – *Adding the value converter resources*
```
<Window.Resources>
    <loc:TitleConverter x:Key="tConv"/>
    <loc:DirtyStarConverter x:Key="dConv"/>
</Window.Resources>
```

Loading the EditingModule module
If we run the application at this point we won't be able to do anything. There will be no documents opened and no active commands. We need to load our module assembly into the application. We will use a directory sweep in order to load the module. The directory that will contain the module assembly will be named "Modules" and it will be placed under the Shell's executable path. We will

create a module catalog that will search this directory and load any modules in the assemblies it finds there. The code in listing 5.11 shows the bootstrapper method override that does this.

Listing 5.11 – *Creating the module catalog*
```
protected override IModuleCatalog CreateModuleCatalog()
{
    return new DirectoryModuleCatalog() { ModulePath = @"Modules" };
}
```

In order to get the EditingModule assembly to the correct location we will need to change its build location or add a post build event that copies the binaries to the desired location. We will choose the first option. Go to the Build properties for the EditingModule project and change the output path to look like the one in figure 5.2. The first part of the path depends on the name of the Shell project so it might differ in your case.

Figure 5.2 – *Changing the project output path*

After you change the output path, build the EditingModule project explicitly so the files get moved. By default the EditingModule project will not be built by VisualStudio. This is because this is not the active project and the active project (the Shell project) does not have a reference on it. You can change this by modifying the Shell project dependencies since all projects are in the same solution.

Open the solution properties and select Project Dependencies in the left pane. Make sure the Shell project is selected in the right pane and check the EditingModule project as a dependency. This can be seen in figure 5.3.

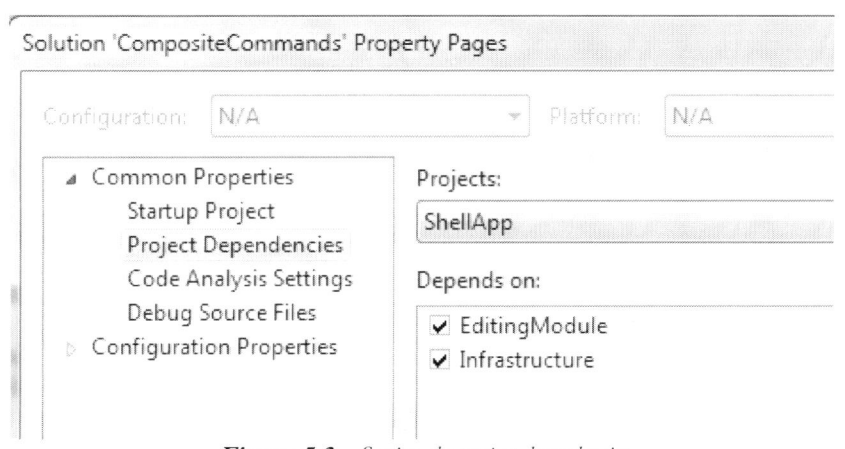

Figure 5.3 – *Setting the project dependencies*

Defining the editing module

In order to actually load our views into the main application region we need to define the module. Add the class definition in listing 5.12 to the EditingModule project.

Listing 5.12 – *EditingModule module definition*

```
public class EditingModule : IModule
{
    private IRegionManager regionManager;
    private IUnityContainer container;
    public EditingModule(IUnityContainer container)
    {
        this.container = container;
        this.regionManager = container.Resolve<IRegionManager>();
    }
    public void Initialize()
    {
        IRegion region = regionManager.Regions["MainRegion"];
        for (int i = 0; i < 3; i++)
        {
            var vm = container.Resolve<DocumentViewModel>();
            vm.Content = "document content";
            var view = new DocumentView();
            view.DataContext = vm;

            region.Add(view);
            region.Activate(view);
        }
    }
}
```

The EditingModule class implements the IModule interface. This tells PRISM that this is a module definition. The module definition uses constructor injection to obtain a reference to the Unity container. In a normal situation injecting a DI container would not be a good decision because we would be using the container as a service locator. The main problem with the service locator is that it hides a class' dependencies possibly introducing runtime errors. This is why the service locator is considered, by some, to be an anti-pattern. I think injecting the Unity container will not do any harm here since we are only using it in the module root to create all other object instances (the DocumentViewModel calss will have dependencies later on).

The IRegionManager service is used, at initialization time, to obtain the region into which the 3 views will be loaded. This is done by using view injection with the IRegion.Add method. After the view is added it is also activated. This will make sure the last opened document is the active one.

Defining the document view

The DocumentView user control has a very simple definition. The XAML below presents it.

```
<TextBox TextWrapping="Wrap" Text="{Binding Content, Mode=TwoWay,
    UpdateSourceTrigger=PropertyChanged}" FontSize="{Binding Size}"/>
```

The view binds to the view-model Content property in order to display the document text. It also binds to the view-model Size property in order to increase or decrease the text size.

Defining the document view-model

As was seen in the definition of the application Shell, the DocumentViewModel view-model also exposes two other properties: the document title and the dirty flag. The view-model's four property definitions can be seen in listing 5.13. The properties' backing fields aren't shown.

Listing 5.13 – *View-model property definitions*
```
public string Title
{
    get { return title; }
    set
    {
        if (title == value) return;
        title = value;
        RaisePropertyChanged("Title");
    }
}
public string Content
{
    get { return content; }
    set
    {
        if (content == value) return;
        content = value;
        RaisePropertyChanged("Content");
        IsDirty = true;
    }
}
public bool IsDirty
{
    get { return isDirty; }
    set
    {
        isDirty = value;
        RaisePropertyChanged("IsDirty");
        saveCmd.RaiseCanExecuteChanged();
    }
}
public int Size
{
    get { return size; }
    set
    {
        if (size == value) return;
        size = value;
        RaisePropertyChanged("Size");
        zinCmd.RaiseCanExecuteChanged();
        zoutCmd.RaiseCanExecuteChanged();
```

```
        IsDirty = true;
    }
}
```

When the Content property changes, the document is marked as dirty. This also happens if the font size changes. When the font size changes, the zoom-in and zoom-out commands raise their CanExecuteChanged events. This allows the view to properly display the commands' status. When the IsDirty flag changes, the save command CanExecuteChanged event is triggered.

Registering the commands
Listing 5.14 presents the DocumentViewModel view-model initialization logic.

Listing 5.14 – *DocumentViewModel initialization code*
```
public class DocumentViewModel:NotificationObject
{
    private const int MIN_SZ = 10, MAX_SZ = 20;

    private DelegateCommand saveCmd, zinCmd, zoutCmd;

    public DocumentViewModel()
    {
        saveCmd = new DelegateCommand(OnSave, CanSave);
        zinCmd = new DelegateCommand(OnZoomIn, CanZoomIn);
        zoutCmd = new DelegateCommand(OnZoomOut, CanZoomOut);

        GlobalCommands.SaveAllCommand.RegisterCommand(saveCmd);
        GlobalCommands.SaveCommand.RegisterCommand(saveCmd);
        GlobalCommands.ZoomInCommand.RegisterCommand(zinCmd);
        GlobalCommands.ZoomOutCommand.RegisterCommand(zoutCmd);

        Size = MIN_SZ;

    }
    ...
}
```

The constructor defines local save, zoom-in and zoom-out commands and registers them with the global composite commands defined in the Infrastructure project. You can also notice that the save command is registered with both the GlobalCommands.SaveAllCommand command and the GlobalCommands.SaveCommand command. This is because we need to support both saving individual documents and saving all documents at the same time. Listing 5.15 presents the handlers for these commands.

Listing 5.15 – *Local command handlers*
```
private void OnSave() { IsDirty = false; }
private bool CanSave() { return IsDirty; }

private void OnZoomIn() { Size += 1; }
private bool CanZoomIn() { return Size < MAX_SZ; }
```

```csharp
private void OnZoomOut() { Size -= 1; }
private bool CanZoomOut() { return Size > MIN_SZ; }
```

Custom CompositeCommands

Running the application at this point will show the 3 opened documents. We can change the content for each one and use the SaveAllCommand command only when all 3 documents are dirty. This is the default CompositeCommand behavior. By default, for a CompositeCommand to be able to execute, all contained commands that are active need to be able to be executed. This can be changed by implementing a custom CompositeCommand class and overriding the CanExecute method. Add the class definition in listing 5.16 to the Infrastructure project.

Listing 5.16 – *Custom composite command definition*
```csharp
public class CustomCompositeCommand:CompositeCommand
{
    public CustomCompositeCommand() : base() { }
    public CustomCompositeCommand(bool monitorCommandActivity)
            : base(monitorCommandActivity) { }
    public override bool CanExecute(object parameter)
    {
        ICommand[] commandList;
        bool hasEnabledCommandsThatShouldBeExecuted = false;
        lock (this.RegisteredCommands)
        {
            commandList = this.RegisteredCommands.ToArray();
        }
        foreach (ICommand command in commandList)
        {
            if (this.ShouldExecute(command))
            {
                if (command.CanExecute(parameter))
                {
                    hasEnabledCommandsThatShouldBeExecuted = true;
                }
            }
        }
        return hasEnabledCommandsThatShouldBeExecuted;
    }
}
```

This implementation enables the CompositeCommand even if at least one child command can be executed. This introduces a slight problem because, at this point, commands will be executed even if their CanExecute method returns false. To fix this we need to check the command execution status before executing each individual command. Add the Execute method override shown in listing 5.17 to the CustomCompositeCommand implementation presented earlier.

Listing 5.17 – *The custom composite command Execute method*
```csharp
public override void Execute(object parameter)
{
    Queue<ICommand> commands;
```

```
        lock (this.RegisteredCommands)
        {
            commands = new Queue<ICommand>(this.RegisteredCommands
              .Where(this.ShouldExecute).ToList());
        }
        while (commands.Count > 0)
        {
            ICommand command = commands.Dequeue();
            if (command.CanExecute(parameter))
                command.Execute(parameter);
        }
    }
```

This CustomCompositeCommand implementation is based 90% on the original implementation offered by the PRISM framework. To apply the new functionality you can change the SaveAllCommand type in the GlobalCommands class from the CompositeCommand type to the CustomCompositeCommand type.

Implementing IActiveAware

The other three implemented commands (Save, ZoomIn and ZoomOut) won't work because the composite commands to which they are registered monitor the command activity. For these commands to work, the registered commands need to be activated. We can do this by implementing the IActiveAware interface in our DocumentViewModel class.

The interface exposes 2 members: the IsActive property and the IsActiveChanged event. The IsActive property will be automatically set by the region adapter when the region's active view changes. This interface can be implemented either in the view or in the view-model. The region adapter checks the view first and if the interface is not implemented there it then checks the view-model. When the IsActive property is changed, we set the active state for the commands and raise the IsActiveChanged event. Add the IActiveAware implementation presented in listing 5.18 to the DocumentViewModel class.

Listing 5.18 – *IActiveAware interface implementation*
```
private bool isActive;
public bool IsActive
{
    get { return isActive; }
    set
    {
        if (isActive == value) return;
        isActive = value;
        RaisePropertyChanged("IsActive");
        saveCmd.IsActive = isActive;
        zinCmd.IsActive = isActive;
        zoutCmd.IsActive = isActive;
        if (IsActiveChanged != null)
            IsActiveChanged(this, EventArgs.Empty);
    }
}
public event EventHandler IsActiveChanged;
```

Running the application now, you should see a window similar to the one presented in figure 5.4. You can use all 4 commands, but there is still a little more to go before the application is finished.

Figure 5.4 – *The main application window*

Unregistering commands

To see how to unregister the commands we will implement a document closing feature. Each document will have a close button. When the button is pressed we unregister the commands and remove the view from the region. Add the command and event presented in listing 5.19 to the DocumentViewModel class.

Listing 5.19 – *Closing the documents*
```
private DelegateCommand closeCmd;
public DelegateCommand CloseCommand { get { return closeCmd; } }
public event EventHandler DocumentClosing;
```

The OnClose handler for this close command can be seen in listing 5.20.

Listing 5.20 – *The Close command handler*
```
private void OnClose()
{
    GlobalCommands.SaveAllCommand.UnregisterCommand(saveCmd);
    GlobalCommands.SaveCommand.UnregisterCommand(saveCmd);
    GlobalCommands.ZoomInCommand.UnregisterCommand(zinCmd);
    GlobalCommands.ZoomOutCommand.UnregisterCommand(zoutCmd);

    if (DocumentClosing != null)
        DocumentClosing(this, EventArgs.Empty);
}
```

In the close handler we use the UnregisterCommand method to unregister the 4 commands. This will allow the view-model to be garbage collected since there won't be any references left to it after the view is removed from the region. We then publish the DocumentClosing event. Removing the view from the main region of the application in the view-model isn't a good idea. Instead we let the event subscriber handle the view removal. This will be done in the EditingModule class. The code presented in listing 5.21 shows the event handler as well as the event subscription code in the Initialize method.

Listing 5.21 – *DocumentClosing event handler definition*
```
var vm = container.Resolve<DocumentViewModel>();
vm.DocumentClosing += OnDocumentClosing;
//...
private void OnDocumentClosing(object sender, EventArgs args)
{
    var vm = sender as DocumentViewModel;
    vm.DocumentClosing -= OnDocumentClosing;

    IRegion region = regionManager.Regions["MainRegion"];
    foreach (FrameworkElement view in region.Views)
    {
        if (view.DataContext == vm)
        {
            region.Remove(view); break;
        }
    }
}
```

The first thing that is done is to unsubscribe from the event. After this, the code searches for the view containing the current view-model. If the view is found, it will be removed from the region. The next step is to modify the TabItem header template in the Shell.xaml file, like in listing 5.22, in order to bind the CloseCommand to a UI element.

Listing 5.22 – *TabItem header template definition*
```
<DataTemplate>
  <Grid>
    <Grid.ColumnDefinitions>
      <ColumnDefinition/>
      <ColumnDefinition Width="auto"/>
    </Grid.ColumnDefinitions>
    <StackPanel Orientation="Horizontal">
      <TextBlock Text="{Binding Title, Converter={StaticResource tConv}}"
          Margin="2,0"/>
      <TextBlock Text="{Binding IsDirty, Converter={StaticResource dConv}}"/>
    </StackPanel>
    <Button Content="X" Command="{Binding CloseCommand}"
        Grid.Column="1"/>
  </Grid>
</DataTemplate>
```

Running the application
At this point the application is complete. Running it, we can modify the document content and increase/decrease the font size. We can also close the opened documents. Figure 5.5 presents the final application user interface.

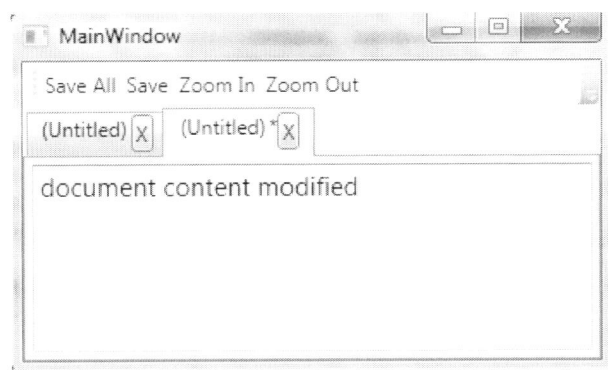

Figure 5.5 – *The application using the new header template*

5.2 Event Aggregators

Another inter-module communication mechanism is represented by PRISM events. The problem with using regular events is that the subscriber needs access to a publisher reference and this introduces unnecessary tight coupling between the modules. To solve this problem, PRISM offers an event mechanism that allows multiple publishers and multiple subscribers to be connected in a loosely coupled fashion. The event itself is the central piece in the interaction, not the publisher. Classes can get a particular event by using the IEventAggregator.GetEvent<T> method and then decide whether to publish the event or subscribe to it.

PRISM events are strongly typed events that derive from the CompositePresentationEvent<T> base class. The generic argument represents the payload type. This is the type of the data that will be passed around between the communicating view-models.

In this section we will continue to work on the document editing application in order to showcase what can be done with the PRISM events. For this section we will try to move the document creation logic from the EditingModule project into the Shell project. The Shell will publish an event with the newly created document. The EditingModule will subscribe to the event and will display the document. The following sections describe the changes to the application.

Creating the PRISM event

The PRISM event we'll use will pass document data between modules. This document data will contain the document title and content. Add the model class presented in listing 5.23 to the Infrastructure project.

Listing 5.23 – *DocumentInfo class definition*
```
public class DocumentInfo
{
    public string Title { get; set; }
    public string Content { get; set; }
}
```

Now we are ready to create our PRISM event. Add the event definition presented in listing 5.24 to the Infrastructure project.

Listing 5.24 – *The composite presentation event definition*
```
public class OpenDocumentEvent:CompositePresentationEvent<DocumentInfo>
{ }
```

You can see that the event has a very simple definition. The event derives from the CompositePresentationEvent class and has a DocumentInfo type that represents its payload. The CompositePresentationEvent base class contains the necessary methods to publish and subscribe to the event as well as to unsubscribe from it.

Subscriber references can be held either with a weak reference or with a strong reference. This is determined at subscription time. If the subscriber chooses to use a strong reference, it must explicitly unsubscribe from the event when the view-model is disposed.

Publishing PRISM events

We will publish the event from the Shell project. For this we need a view-model and a new command bound to a toolbar button. When the button is pressed, a DocumentInfo instance is created and published using the IEventAggregator service. Add the class definition presented in listing 5.25 to the Shell project. This Shell view-model uses constructor injection to obtain a reference to the event aggregator service.

Listing 5.25 – *The ShellViewModel class definition*
```
public class ShellViewModel
{
    private DelegateCommand newCmd;
    private IEventAggregator eventAggregator;

    public ShellViewModel(IEventAggregator eventAggregator)
    {
        this.eventAggregator = eventAggregator;
        newCmd = new DelegateCommand(OnNew);
    }

    public DelegateCommand NewCommand { get { return newCmd; } }

    private void OnNew()
    {
        var doc = new DocumentInfo() { Content = "document content" };

        eventAggregator.GetEvent<OpenDocumentEvent>()
            .Publish(doc);
    }
}
```

The PRISM event is published using the Publish method. This method accepts a single argument of the DocumentInfo type. This will be the payload that will be used by the subscriber to open the document.

Binding the Shell view-model

After the view-model is created we need to link it to the Shell view and also bind the NewCommand

command to a toolbar button. Modify the bootstrapper InitializeShell method like in listing 5.26. You can see that the view-model is resolved from the Unity container in order to satisfy the IEventAggregator dependency.

Listing 5.26 – *Initializing the shell*
```
protected override void InitializeShell()
{
    var view=(AppShell)this.Shell;
    view.DataContext = Container.Resolve<ShellViewModel>();
    App.Current.MainWindow = view;
    App.Current.MainWindow.Show();
}
```

Add a new toolbar button and bind it to the view-model command as below.

```
<Button Content="New" Command="{Binding NewCommand}" Margin="4,0"/>
```

Subscribing to the PRISM event

In order to subscribe to a PRISM event, we use the Subscribe method exposed by the CompositePresentationEvent<T> instance. Such an instance is obtained by calling the event aggregator's GetEvent<T> method.

We subscribe to the OpenDocumentEvent event in the EditingModule project. The best option for this application is to do this from the module class definition. Modify the module Initialize method as shown in listing 5.27.

Listing 5.27 – *The module initialization code*
```
public void Initialize()
{
    IEventAggregator evtAggregator = container.Resolve<IEventAggregator>();
    evtAggregator.GetEvent<OpenDocumentEvent>()
        .Subscribe(OnOpenDocument, ThreadOption.UIThread);
}
```

The Initialization method gets a reference to the IEventAggregator service. It will use this reference to subscribe to the OpenDocumentEvent event when the module is initialized. A couple of things are worth mentioning here. The handler needs to be public. Also, notice that I specified that the handler should be called on the UI thread. This is necessary since the UI can only be updated from the UI thread.

The ThreadOption enumeration specifies the thread the subscriber handler is executed on. We have the following options: UIThread, PublisherThread and BackgroundThread. The UIThread option executes the handler on the UI thread. The PublisherThread option executes the handler on the same thread as the event publisher. This is the default option. The BackgroundThread option executes the handler on a background thread from the thread pool. Listing 5.28 shows the definition for the OnOpenDocument handler.

Listing 5.28 – *OnOpenDocument event handler definition*
```
public void OnOpenDocument(DocumentInfo doc)
```

```
{
    var vm = container.Resolve<DocumentViewModel>();
    vm.Content = doc.Content;
    vm.Title = doc.Title;
    vm.DocumentClosing += OnDocumentClosing;
    var view = new DocumentView();
    view.DataContext = vm;
    IRegion region = regionManager.Regions["MainRegion"];
    region.Add(view);
    region.Activate(view);
}
```

The application is almost complete. Try running it and see what happens. You can add a few documents and things go wrong after you close them all. Remember what I said about event aggregator subscriber references being weak references by default? Since the ModuleManager does not hold a reference to the module definition, this might go out of scope and be garbage collected at any time after initialization. The IEventAggregator service doesn't hold a reference to it either. We need to change this by specifying that we want hard references. Change the EditingModule.Initialize method code, like below.

```
eventAggregator.GetEvent<OpenDocumentEvent>()
    .Subscribe(OnOpenDocument, ThreadOption.UIThread, true);
```

Now, the IEventAggregator service holds a reference to the subscriber and we'll be able to add and close as many documents as we want. There is no need to unsubscribe from the event in this situation. The module is loaded for the entire duration of the application. When we close the application, all resources will be released.

Unsubscribing from events

Other situations require us to unsubscribe from a particular event. This is the case when a view-model subscribes to an event with a hard reference and the view-model needs to be disposed of. Before releasing the resources we need to make sure we unsubscribe from the event so that the view-model can be garbage collected. This can be done using the Unsubscribe method, like below.

```
eventAggregator.GetEvent<OpenDocumentEvent>()
    .Unsubscribe(OnOpenDocument);
```

The Unsubscribe method also has an overload that accepts a SubscriptionToken instance. This token is returned by every Subscribe method call. We can use this overload when we subscribe multiple times to the same event using the same handler. This might be used to disable a particular subscription filter.

Filtering events

One other overload of the Subscribe method accepts a Predicate<T> delegate. The subscriber handler won't be called unless this filter method returns true. An example of this can be seen in listing 5.29.

Listing 5.29 – *Filtering composite presentation events*
```
public void Initialize()
{
    IEventAggregator evtAggregator = container.Resolve<IEventAggregator>();

    eventAggregator.GetEvent<OpenDocumentEvent>()
        .Subscribe(OnOpenDocument, ThreadOption.UIThread, true, OnFilter);
}
private bool OnFilter(DocumentInfo doc)
{
    if (docCount >= 3)
        return false;
    return true;
}
```

This code allows us to create only 3 documents at a time. The counter will be incremented after each view is shown in the OnOpenDocument method. The counter will be decremented after each view is removed in the OnDocumentClosing event handler.

The event aggregator use case presented in this sample application isn't very useful but it presents the way the PRISM events should be used. A more realistic use case would include a master-detail composite view. The master view-model, implemented in one module, can send an event, containing the currently selected item, to the details view-model, implemented in another module. When the details view-model receives the event it can download and show the data.

A concrete example can include a master view that displays a list of customers. When a customer is selected in the view, the master view-model publishes an event with the selected customer as the payload. When the details view-model receives the event it can download a list of orders for the selected customer and display it through the details view.

5.3 Shared Services

The last inter module communication option we will talk about is shared services. These are services that are used by multiple modules but are defined in a single module. One example of such a service might be a user interaction service.

The service interface can be defined in the Infrastructure project, in order for the service to be accessible from the entire application, while the implementation can be defined in the Shell project. The Shell could then register the service and allow it to be used everywhere.

Defining the service interface

In order to see this in action we will add a shared service in order to save our documents to disk. Add the service interface from listing 5.30 to the Infrastructure project.

Listing 5.30 – *The IInteractionService interface definition*
```
public interface IInteractionService
{
    void SaveFile(DocumentInfo doc, Action<Exception> callback);
}
```

This service will be called from the EditingModule's DocumentViewModel view-model class.

An exception will be returned in the callback if there was a problem while saving the document. You can see that this service has a callback interface. This is in order to not enforce a synchronous calling pattern. This service can thus be easily reused in a Silverlight project.

Implementing the service

Add the implementation of this service from listing 5.31 to the Shell project. You can see that the implementation uses a blocking call to the SaveFileDialog.ShowDialog method. The callback is called after the file is saved. Also because the blocking call is abstracted behind the callback interface, this code can be changed to use a Silverlight ChildWindow instance for example.

Listing 5.31 – *The InteractionService service implementation*
```
public class InteractionService:IInteractionService
{
    public void SaveFile(DocumentInfo document, Action<Exception> callback)
    {
        if (string.IsNullOrEmpty(document.Title))
        {
            SaveFileDialog dlg = new SaveFileDialog();
            dlg.Filter = "text files (*.txt)|*.txt";

            bool? res = dlg.ShowDialog();
            if (res.HasValue && res.Value)
            {
                document.Title = dlg.FileName;
            }
            else { return; }
        }
        try
        {
            Save(document);
            callback(null);
        }
        catch (Exception ex)
        {
            callback(ex);
        }
    }
    private void Save(DocumentInfo document)
    {
        using (var sw = new StreamWriter(document.Title, false))
        {
            sw.Write(document.Content);
        }
    }
}
```

Registering the service

The next step is to expose the service to the entire application. This can be done by registering the service with the Unity container. Add the method override from listing 5.32 to the bootstrapper code. Also, make sure to keep the base ConfigureContainer call. This will register the default PRISM services.

Listing 5.32 – *Registering the interaction service*
```
protected override void ConfigureContainer()
{
    base.ConfigureContainer();
    Container.RegisterInstance<IInteractionService>(new InteractionService());
}
```

Saving the documents

In order to save the documents we need to use the IInteractionService service from the DocumentViewModel class. The service instance will be supplied through constructor injection. This can be seen in listing 5.33.

Listing 5.33 – *Injecting the interaction service into the view-model*
```
public DocumentViewModel(IInteractionService intService)
{
    this.intService = intService;
}
```

To save the current document, modify the OnSave handler as listing 5.34 shows.

Listing 5.34 – *Saving the current document*
```
private void OnSave()
{
    var doc = new DocumentInfo() { Title = Title, Content = Content };
    intService.SaveFile(doc, ex =>
    {
        if (ex == null)
        {
            IsDirty = false;
            Title = doc.Title;
            return;
        }
        //handle exception
    });
}
```

Running the application now will allow you to save the documents to disk. Logic can also be added to open existing documents.

5.4 Summary

Even if an application is composed of independently developed modules, these modules still need to communicate with each other in order for the application to function correctly. In this chapter we saw 3 options that we have in order to communicate between modules in a loosely coupled manner. Our first option is to use composite commands. A composite command is an ICommand implementation that allows us to execute multiple commands at once. The composite commands will be defined in the infrastructure assembly. Modules can then register local commands with the composite command in order to have their code run whenever the global composite command is run.

The second communication mechanism is represented by event aggregators. This is the recommended way of communicating between view-models. Multiple view-models can publish an event and other view-models can subscribe to these events. Event handlers can be invoked on a background thread or on the UI thread and can also be filtered.

The last communication option that was presented was represented by shared services. These are services whose interface is declared in the infrastructure assembly. In this way they can be accessed from every module. The service implementation is local to the defining module or Shell.Insert chapter five text here.

CHAPTER 6: REGIONS

Regions are named placeholders that can be used to add content to a view at runtime. Regions are similar to ASP.NET content placeholders. Regions can contain 0 or multiple views. These views can be displayed one at a time or all at once, depending on the UI element that is used to host the region. For example, if the region is hosted in a ContentControl, only a single view in that region will be displayed at any one time. If the region is hosted in an ItemsControl, all views in that region are displayed at the same time.

Regions allow you to decouple the views that need to be shown from their position on the screen. Modules can contribute views to regions without knowing where those views will be displayed.

6.1 Defining regions

PRISM regions are represented by the IRegion interface. The interface definition can be seen in listing 6.1.

Listing 6.1 – *The IRegion interface definition*
```
public interface IRegion : INavigateAsync, INotifyPropertyChanged
{
    IViewsCollection Views { get; }
    IViewsCollection ActiveViews { get; }
    object Context { get; set; }
    string Name { get; set; }
    Comparison<object> SortComparison { get; set; }
    IRegionManager Add(object view);
    IRegionManager Add(object view, string viewName);
    IRegionManager Add(object view, string viewName,
        bool createRegionManagerScope);
    void Remove(object view);
    void Activate(object view);
    void Deactivate(object view);
    object GetView(string viewName);
    IRegionManager RegionManager { get; set; }
    IRegionBehaviorCollection Behaviors { get; }
```

```
    IRegionNavigationService NavigationService { get; set; }
}
```

Each region exposes 2 collections of views. One collection holds all the views that are hosted in the region while the other contains only the active views. Each region has a name and a context. The name is used to uniquely identify the region within its region manager and the context is used to share data between all the region's views.

The Add methods are used to add views to the region. There is an option to add named view, that can later be retrieved, and also an option to create a scoped region manager while adding a view. This is useful if we want to add multiple instances of the same view to a region and that view defines its own region.

The region also offers the possibility to remove views, through the Remove method, and to retrieve a named view. Views inside a region can be activated or deactivated. These operations are relevant only when the region is not hosted in an ItemsControl.

A region manager is responsible for creating and maintaining a collection of regions. The region manager uses region adapters in order to create regions and to attach them to a particular control. By default, PRISM offers 4 region adapters.

The ContentControlRegionAdapter adapter is used to associate a region with a ContentControl. The region that is associated is a SingleActiveRegion instance. This implementation of the IRegion interface allows a single active view at any one time. The SingleActiveRegion implementation derives from the Region class and overrides the Activate method in order to activate the supplied region and deactivate the previous active region.

The ItemsControlRegionAdapter adapter is used to associate a region with an ItemsControl. The region that is associated is an AllActiveRegion instance. In this implementation of the IRegion interface all views are active. The AllActiveRegion implementation derives from the Region class and overrides the ActiveViews collection in order to return all views.

The SelectorRegionAdapter adapter is used to associate a region with a Selector control. The region that is associated is a Region instance. This implementation of the IRegion interface allows multiple active views.

The TabControlRegionAdapter adapter is used to associate a region with a TabControl control. This adapter is used only in Silverlight. This is because the Silverlight TabControl doesn't derive from the Selector class. This region adapter also offers an attached property that allows us to set the Style for each TabItem. This is done by using the ItemContainerStyle attached property.

Views can be added to a region in 2 ways: view discovery and view injection.

6.2 View discovery

With view discovery, modules register views with a particular region. When that region is displayed, the views will automatically be added to the region and shown in the UI. With view discovery you do not have control over when the views are created and added to the region. View discovery can be used in cases where the views in a region don't change during the application lifetime. This can be the case when building an application menu where each module registers its corresponding menu items to a menu region. In order to use view discovery we can use the RegisterViewWithRegion method from the RegionManager class as below.

```
regionManager.RegisterViewWithRegion("CustomerDetailsRegion", typeof(DetailsView));
```

The first method argument represents the region name while the second is the type of view we want to register with the region. If the view needs special configuration before being registered with the region we can use a second method overload that accepts a delegate. This delegate returns the view instance that will be registered with the region. This can be seen below.

```
regionManager.RegisterViewWithRegion("ControlPanelRegion", () =>
    new CommandViewModel("Customers", new DelegateCommand(OnProducts)));
```

The RegisterViewWithRegion method is a RegionManager extension method defined in the RegionManagerExtensions class. One of the method definitions can be seen in listing 6.2.

Listing 6.2 – *The RegisterViewWithRegion extension method*
```
public static IRegionManager RegisterViewWithRegion(
        this IRegionManager regionManager, string regionName, Type viewType)
{
    var regionViewRegistry = ServiceLocator
        .Current.GetInstance<IRegionViewRegistry>();
    regionViewRegistry.RegisterViewWithRegion(regionName, viewType);
    return regionManager;
}
```

You can see that the method actually registers the view with the RegionViewRegistry and returns the region manager that was used to call the method. All views added through view discovery will use the ambient region manager. The RegionViewRegistry is used to map view instances to region names. When a region is displayed, the region searches this registry for all views that were registered to it. The region retrieves these views and populates itself. The RegisterViewWithRegion method definition from the RegionViewRegistry class is presented in listing 6.3.

Listing 6.3 – *The region view registry definition for RegisterViewWithRegion*
```
public void RegisterViewWithRegion(string regionName, Type viewType)
{
    this.RegisterViewWithRegion(regionName,
        () => this.CreateInstance(viewType));
}
public void RegisterViewWithRegion(string regionName,
        Func<object> getContentDelegate)
{
    this.registeredContent.Add(regionName, getContentDelegate);
    this.OnContentRegistered(new ViewRegisteredEventArgs(
        regionName, getContentDelegate));
}
```

You can see that the registry actually maps region names to delegates that are used to retrieve the content. This ensures that the views are created only if necessary. The region populates itself with the views by calling the RegionViewRegistry.GetContents method. This method is called from the AutoPopulateRegionBehavior behavior. This behavior was specifically created to support view discovery. The GetContents method definition can be seen in listing 6.4.

Listing 6.4 – *Retrieving all views registered with a region*
```
public IEnumerable<object> GetContents(string regionName)
{
    List<object> items = new List<object>();
    foreach (Func<object> getContentDelegate in this.registeredContent[regionName])
    {
        items.Add(getContentDelegate());
    }
    return items;
}
```

6.3 View injection

View injection is the process of adding views to a region in code. With view injection you have full control over when the views are created and displayed in the region. View injection is used in cases where the region views change often. This might be the case of a document editing application that presents a tabbed region that is used to edit the documents. The documents can be added to this region via view injection. View injection can also be used when we need to inject multiple instances of the same view inside a region, with different arguments. In order to use view injection we will need a reference to the region into which we want to inject the views. This is done by querying the region manager. Once we have the region instance we can use one of the Add method overloads to inject our views. Listing 6.5 shows an example.

Listing 6.5 – *Adding a view with view injection*
```
IRegion region = regionManager.Regions["MainRegion"];
region.Add(container.Resolve<CustomersView>(), "CustomersView");
```

The first method argument represents the view that will be injected while the second is the name of the registration. Injecting named views is helpful if we later want to retrieve and remove the view from the region. Retrieving a named view can be done by using the Region.GetView method. With view injection we also have the possibility to remove views from a particular region. This can be seen in listing 6.6.

Listing 6.6 – *Removing a view from a region*
```
IRegion region = regionManager.Regions["MainRegion"];
object view = region.GetView("CustomersView");
region.Remove(view);
```

There are times when we need to create multiple instances of a view and that view contains a region. In these cases we need to create a separate region manager for the contained regions.

These types of scenarios are supported only for view injection. View injection offers the possibility to create a new region manager when adding a view to a region. This region manager is used to manage the regions contained within the added view.

When using view discovery all regions are added to a parent region manager which is usually the global region manager that was registered in the shell. Since the region manager uses the region name to uniquely identify regions, region names must be unique within the same region manager. If we try to create 2 regions with the same name with view discovery, PRISM will throw an exception. The code in listing 6.7 presents how to specify that we want a new region manager.

Listing 6.7 – *Creating a new region manager to manage the regions inside the added view*
```
IRegion region = regionManager.Regions["MainRegion"];
IRegionManager mgr = region.Add(container.Resolve<CustomersView>(),
    "CustomersView", true);
```

After this code runs, all regions contained by the view will receive the new region manager. Whether it uses view discovery or view injection, an application might want to sort the views that appear in a particular region. This sorting can be done by using the ViewSortHintAttribute attribute. This attribute provides a Hint property of type string that is used for sorting inside the region. Listing 6.8 shows an example of how this attribute can be applied on a view.

Listing 6.8 – *Sorting views inside a region*
```
[ViewSortHint("01")]
public class OrdersViewModel:NotificationObject, IRegionContextAware
[ViewSortHint("02")]
public class DetailsViewModel:NotificationObject, IRegionContextAware
```

If we need to sort the views by something other than a string we can assign our custom sort comparison. Listing 6.9 shows an example.

Listing 6.9 – *Applying custom view sorting*
```
IRegion region = regionManager.Regions["MainRegion"];
region.SortComparison = (obj1, obj2) =>
{
    return 0;
};
```

This custom comparison can even allow you to sort views based on view-model data even if you are using a view-first approach.

6.4 Building a region based application

In order to showcase the PRISM region support we will build a sample application. The application will present some customers and their orders as well as a list of products. The finished application can be seen in figure 6.1.

Application architecture

The application Shell will contain 2 regions. One region, the ControlPanelRegion region, will be used to display a menu while the other, the MainRegion region, will be used to display the main content based on the selected link. Figure 6.2 presents the 2 regions.

The application functionality is provided by 2 modules that will be loaded via directory sweeping. When a module is initialized it will register a view with the ControlPanelRegion region. This will be done via view discovery. When the user clicks a link in the menu, content will be loaded into the MainRegion region. This will be achieved via view injection. We will also have an infrastructure assembly that will be used to hold the common types used by the modules. Figure 6.3

presents the application architecture.

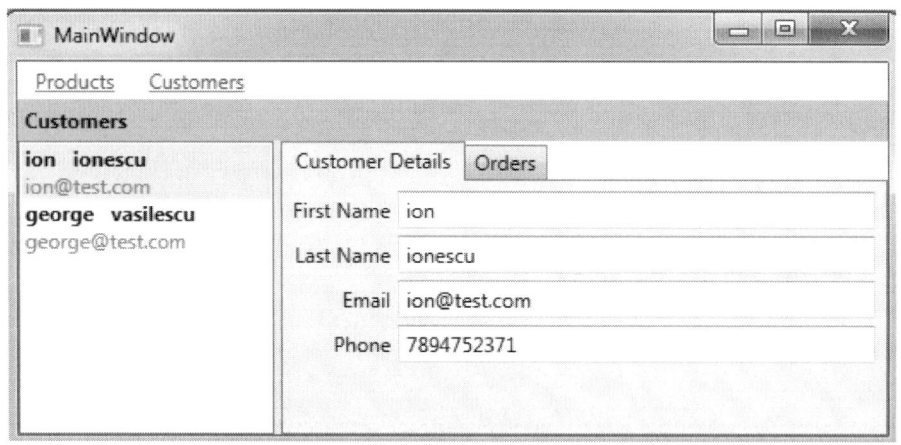

Figure 6.1 – *The finished application user interface*

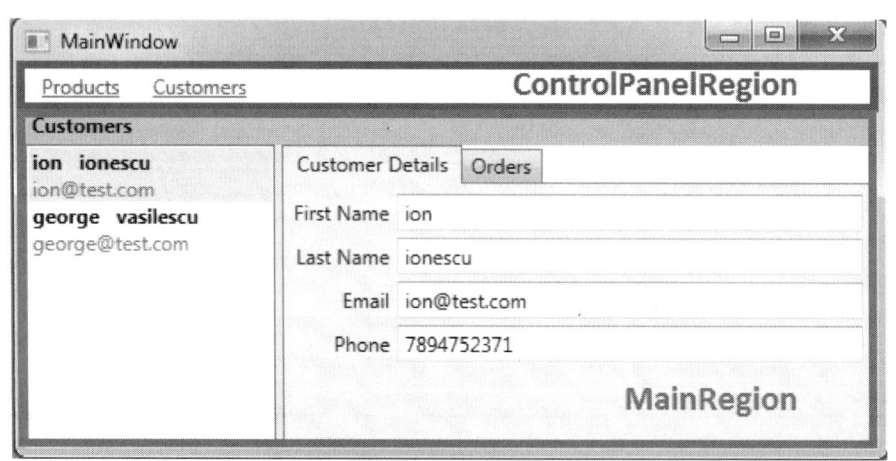

Figure 6.2 – *The Shell regions*

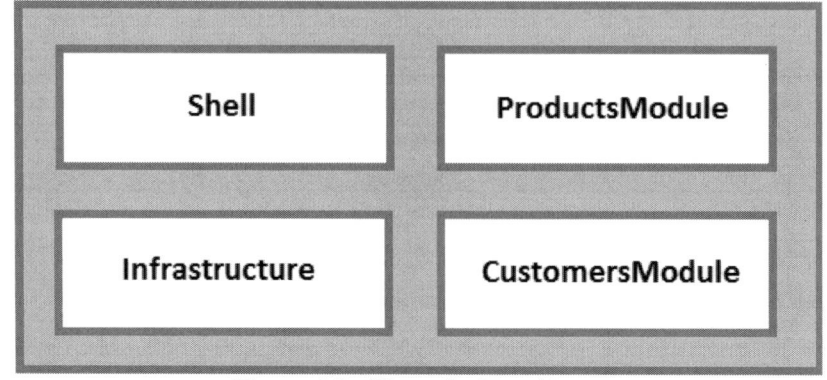

Figure 6.3 – *The application architecture*

Creating the application wireframe

Create a new WPF application project and name it Regions. This will be the Shell assembly. Add the PRISM assemblies that use Unity as a DI container. Add the class definition presented in listing 6.10 to the Shell project to define the application bootstrapper.

Listing 6.10 – *The application bootstrapper definition*
```
public class Bootstrapper : UnityBootstrapper
{
    protected override DependencyObject CreateShell()
    {
        return new MainWindow();
    }
    protected override void InitializeShell()
    {
        base.InitializeShell();
        var shell = Shell as MainWindow;
        App.Current.MainWindow = shell;
        shell.Show();
    }
}
```

Delete the StartupUri property from the App.xaml file and add the method override, presented in listing 6.11, to the App.xaml.cs file, in order to start the bootstrapper.

Listing 6.11 – *The application initialization code*
```
protected override void OnStartup(StartupEventArgs e)
{
    base.OnStartup(e);
    new Bootstrapper().Run();
}
```

Creating regions in XAML is done by setting the RegionManager.RegionName attached property on a ContentControl or an ItemsControl derived UI element. Add an XML prefix for the PRISM assemblies and add the XAML presented in listing 6.12 to the MainWindow.xaml file.

Listing 6.12 – *The shell XAML definition*
```xml
<Grid.RowDefinitions>
    <RowDefinition Height="auto"/>
    <RowDefinition/>
</Grid.RowDefinitions>
<ItemsControl p:RegionManager.RegionName="ControlPanelRegion">
    <ItemsControl.ItemsPanel>
        <ItemsPanelTemplate>
            <StackPanel Orientation="Horizontal"/>
        </ItemsPanelTemplate>
    </ItemsControl.ItemsPanel>
    <ItemsControl.ItemTemplate>
        <DataTemplate>
            <TextBlock Margin="10,3">
```

```xml
            <Hyperlink Command="{Binding Command, Mode=OneWay}">
                <Run Text="{Binding DisplayName, Mode=OneWay}"/>
            </Hyperlink>
        </TextBlock>
      </DataTemplate>
    </ItemsControl.ItemTemplate>
</ItemsControl>
<ContentControl p:RegionManager.RegionName="MainRegion" Grid.Row="1"
        HorizontalContentAlignment="Stretch" VerticalContentAlignment="Stretch"/>
```

This XAML will create our 2 regions. The ControlPanelRegion region is hosted in an ItemsControl. We provide a horizontal StackPanel as the items panel template in order to display the commands on a single line. The views that will be hosted in this region will be active all the time and they will be added by using view discovery. The MainRegion region is hosted in a ContentControl. Only one view in this region will be active at any one time. Since the content in this region changes often we will use view injection to add our views.

Add a new WPF User Control Library project to the solution and name it Infrastructure. This project will contain all the common types that will be used in the application. Add a reference to the Microsoft.Practices.Prism.dll assembly. Add the class definition presented in listing 6.13 to the Infrastructure project. This class will be used to represent the application menu items.

Listing 6.13 – *Application menu item class definition*
```csharp
public class CommandViewModel
{
    private string displayName;
    private ICommand command;
    public CommandViewModel(string displayName, ICommand command)
    {
        this.displayName = displayName;
        this.command = command;
    }
    public string DisplayName { get { return displayName; } }
    public ICommand Command { get { return command; } }
}
```

This class will represent the views that will be registered with the ControlPanelRegion region. At initialization time, modules will create an instance of this type and will register it with the specified region in order to form the application menu.

Create 2 new WPF User Control Library projects, one for each module, and name them ProductsModule and CustomersModule respectively. Delete the auto-generated user control files from each project. Make sure to add references to the Microsoft.Practices.Prism.dll and Microsoft.Practices.Unity.dll libraries from both module projects as well as a reference to the Infrastructure project.

Add the class definition presented in listing 6.14 to the ProductsModule project.

Listing 6.14 – *ProductsModule module definition*
```csharp
[Module(ModuleName = "ProductsModule")]
public class Module : IModule
```

```csharp
{
    private IRegionManager regionManager;
    private IUnityContainer container;
    public Module(IRegionManager regionManager, IUnityContainer container)
    {
        this.regionManager = regionManager;
        this.container = container;
    }
    public void Initialize()
    {
        //use view discovery to display the menu item
        regionManager.RegisterViewWithRegion("ControlPanelRegion", () =>
            new CommandViewModel("Products", new DelegateCommand(OnProducts)));
    }
    private void OnProducts() { }
}
```

This class defines the ProductsModule module. You can see that, at initialization time, the module uses the RegionManager.RegisterViewWithRegion method in order to register a CommandViewModel view to the ControlPanelRegion region. This code uses the method overload that accepts a delegate in order to supply the view. The command handler is empty at the moment. We will change this shortly by adding the code that adds a view to the MainRegion region. You can also see that we use the ModuleAttribute attribute in order to specify the module name.

Add the class definition presented in listing 6.15 to the CustomersModule project.

Listing 6.15 – *CustomersModule module definition*
```csharp
[Module(ModuleName = "CustomersModule")]
public class Module : IModule
{
    private IRegionManager regionManager;
    private IUnityContainer container;
    public Module(IRegionManager regionManager, IUnityContainer container)
    {
        this.regionManager = regionManager;
        this.container = container;
    }

    public void Initialize()
    {
        //use view discovery to display the menu item
        regionManager.RegisterViewWithRegion("ControlPanelRegion", () =>
            new CommandViewModel("Customers", new DelegateCommand(OnProducts)));
    }
    private void OnProducts() { }
}
```

This code is almost identical to the one in the ProductsModule module. The only difference is the module name in the attribute and the name of the command.

The next thing we need to do is to load these modules into the Shell application. We do this by using a DirectoryModuleCatalog. Add the method override shown in listing 6.16 to the bootstrapper implementation.

Listing 6.16 – *Creating the module catalog*
```
protected override IModuleCatalog CreateModuleCatalog()
{
    return new DirectoryModuleCatalog() { ModulePath = ".\\Modules" };
}
```

Before we run the app we need to make sure that the Modules directory exists and that it contains the module assemblies. For this we need to change the build output path for each of the module projects. Change the path for each module project to match the one shown in figure 6.4. The first part of the path is the name of the Shell project. Your path could be different.

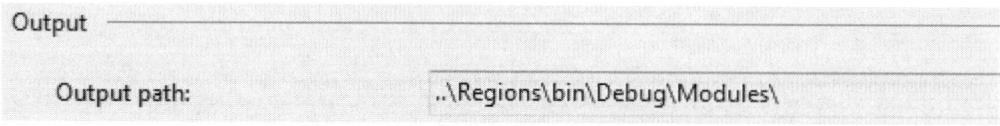

Figure 6.4 – *Setting the project output path*

You also need to make sure that the module projects are built and deployed every time we build the Shell app. This doesn't happen automatically since the Shell application doesn't have any references to the module assemblies. To make this happen we need to explicitly set a dependency on these projects. This can be done in the solution properties window as figure 6.5 shows.

Running the application at this time should display the menu. Clicking the links will have no effect since the command handlers are empty.

The Products View

The products view is an empty view. It is only defined so that you can see changes when the user clicks a different menu item. Add a new user control to the ProductsModule project and name it ProductsView. Add the XAML shown in listing 6.17 to this view.

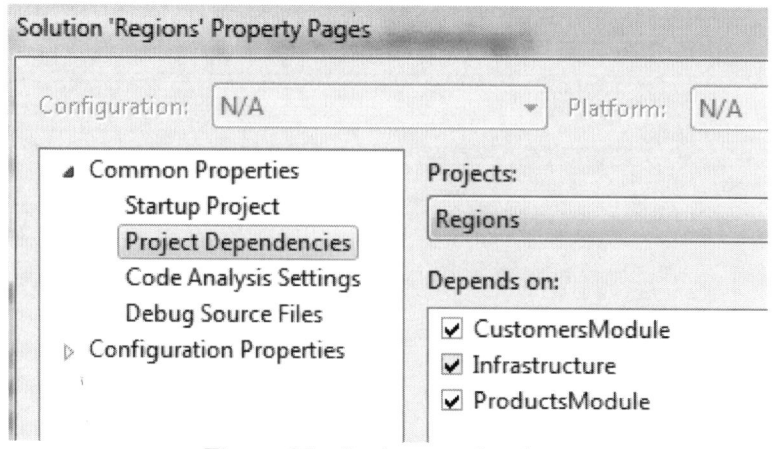

Figure 6.5 – *Set the project dependencies*

Listing 6.17 – *The ProductsView view definition*
```xml
<Grid.RowDefinitions>
    <RowDefinition Height="auto"/>
    <RowDefinition/>
</Grid.RowDefinitions>
<Border Background="LightBlue">
    <TextBlock Text="Products" Margin="4" FontWeight="Bold"/>
</Border>
<Grid Grid.Row="1">
    <TextBlock Text="Demo Products View"
               HorizontalAlignment="Center" VerticalAlignment="Center"
               FontWeight="Bold"/>
</Grid>
```

The only thing left to do is to display this view when the user clicks the correct link. Add the command handler presented in listing 6.18 to the Module class in the ProductsModule project.

Listing 6.18 – *Displaying the products using view injection*
```csharp
private void OnProducts()
{
    //use view injection to display the view in the main region
    IRegion region = regionManager.Regions["MainRegion"];
    object view = region.GetView("ProductsView");
    if (view != null)
        region.Activate(view);
    else
        region.Add(container.Resolve<ProductsView>(), "ProductsView");
}
```

This command handler uses the injected region manager to get a reference to the MainRegion region. After this, it checks to see if the region contains a view named ProductsView. If the view exists it is activated. If the view does not exist it is created and added to the region using view injection. There is no point in creating multiple instances of the same view so activating an already existing view will make sure that view will be the one shown in the ContentControl.

We use view injection to add views to the MainRegion region because we need to have control over the time when the views are added. You can also see that we use the injected unity container to resolve the view. This will make sure that any view dependencies, like a view-model, are created and injected. Instead of activating the existing view, we could have deleted the old view and created a new one from scratch.

The Customers View
The customers view is a little more complicated. This is a composite view that contains 2 more regions. The view can be seen in figure 6.6.

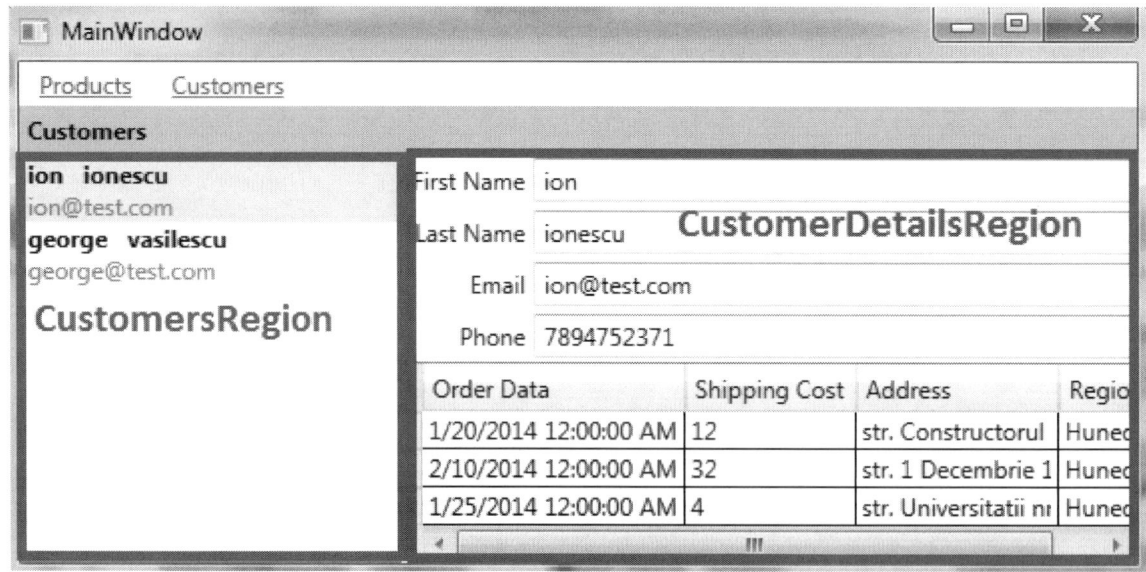

Figure 6.6 – *The CustomersView regions*

Add a new user control to the CustomersModule project and name it CustomersView. The XAML presented in listing 6.19 presents the view content.

Listing 6.19 – *The CustomersView view definition*
```xml
<Grid.RowDefinitions>
    <RowDefinition Height="auto"/>
    <RowDefinition/>
</Grid.RowDefinitions>
<Border Background="LightBlue">
    <TextBlock Text="Customers" Margin="4" FontWeight="Bold"/>
</Border>
<Grid Grid.Row="1">
    <Grid.ColumnDefinitions>
        <ColumnDefinition Width="150"/>
        <ColumnDefinition Width="auto"/>
        <ColumnDefinition Width="*"/>
    </Grid.ColumnDefinitions>
    <ContentControl HorizontalContentAlignment="Stretch"
        VerticalContentAlignment="Stretch"
        p:RegionManager.RegionName="CustomersRegion"/>
    <GridSplitter Grid.Column="1" HorizontalAlignment="Stretch"
                VerticalAlignment="Stretch" Width="4"/>
    <ContentControl HorizontalContentAlignment="Stretch"
        VerticalContentAlignment="Stretch"
        p:RegionManager.RegionName="CustomerDetailsRegion" Grid.Column="2"/>
</Grid>
```

You can see that we define 2 new regions: CustomersRegion and CustomerDetailsRegion. The CustomersRegion region will display the list of customers, while the CustomerDetailsRegion region will display customer details including customer orders. Add the command handler shown in listing 6.20 to the CustomersModule module. This code is similar to what we did for the ProductsModule module.

Listing 6.20 – *Displaying the customers view using view injection*
```
private void OnCustomers()
{
    //use view injection to display the view in the main region
    IRegion region = regionManager.Regions["MainRegion"];
    object view = region.GetView("CustomersView");
    if (view != null)
        region.Activate(view);
    else
        region.Add(container.Resolve<CustomersView>(), "CustomersView");
}
```

The customer service

Before we can display the customer data we need to talk about the service that allows us to get this data. We will define the service interface in the Infrastructure project and we will implement it in the CustomersModule project. We will register the service with the unity container in the customer module initialization code. Add the service interface definition presented in listing 6.21 to the Infrastructure project.

Listing 6.21 – *The customer service interface definition*
```
public interface ICustomerService
{
    List<Customer> GetCustomers();
    Customer GetCustomer(int custId);
    List<Order> GetCustomerOrders(int custId);
}
```

The Customer and Order class definitions can be seen in listing 6.22.

Listing 6.22 – *The Customer and Order class definitions*
```
public class Customer
{
    public int Id { get; set; }
    public string FirstName { get; set; }
    public string LastName { get; set; }
    public string Email { get; set; }
    public string Phone { get; set; }
}
public class Order
{
    public DateTime OrderDate { get; set; }
    public string ShipAddress { get; set; }
    public string ShipRegion { get; set; }
    public decimal ShippingCost { get; set; }
}
```

Add the service implementation presented in listing 6.23 to the CustomersModule project. The code doesn't list all the properties that have been set, only the structure of the data.

Listing 6.23 – *The customer service implementation*
```
public class CustomerService:ICustomerService
{
    private List<Customer> customers;
    private Dictionary<int, List<Order>> orders;
    public CustomerService()
    {
        customers = new List<Customer>(){
            new Customer(){Id=1, FirstName="ion", LastName="ionescu"},
            new Customer(){Id=2, FirstName="george", LastName="georgescu"},
        };
        orders = new Dictionary<int, List<Order>>();
        orders.Add(1, new List<Order>() {
            new Order(){OrderDate=new DateTime(2014, 1, 20)},
            new Order(){OrderDate=new DateTime(2014, 2, 10)},
            new Order(){OrderDate=new DateTime(2014, 1, 25)}});
        orders.Add(2, new List<Order>() {
            new Order(){OrderDate=new DateTime(2014, 1, 20)},
            new Order(){OrderDate=new DateTime(2014, 2, 10)},
        });
    }
    public List<Customer> GetCustomers()
    { return customers; }
    public Customer GetCustomer(int custId)
    { return customers.Where(p => p.Id == custId).SingleOrDefault(); }
    public List<Order> GetCustomerOrders(int custId)
    {
        if (!orders.ContainsKey(custId)) return new List<Order>();
        return orders.Where(p => p.Key == custId).Single().Value;
    }
}
```

Add the following line at the beginning of the module Initialize method. This will register the customer service so that it can be resolved when needed.

```
container.RegisterInstance<ICustomerService>(new CustomerService());
```

Displaying the customer list
Add a new user control to the CustomersModule and name it CustomerListView. The XAML shown in listing 6.24 presents its content. You can see that the view displays the customer list in a list box.

Listing 6.24 – *The customer list view definition*
```
<ListBox ItemsSource="{Binding Customers}" IsSynchronizedWithCurrentItem="True">
    <ListBox.ItemTemplate>
        <DataTemplate>
            <StackPanel>
```

```xml
            <TextBlock FontWeight="Bold">
                <Run Text="{Binding FirstName, Mode=OneWay}"/>
                <Run Text=" "/>
                <Run Text="{Binding LastName, Mode=OneWay}"/>
            </TextBlock>
            <TextBlock Text="{Binding Email}" Foreground="Gray"/>
        </StackPanel>
    </DataTemplate>
</ListBox.ItemTemplate>
</ListBox>
```

The currently selected customer is tracked by using an ICollectionView. In order to keep the ICollectionView synchronized to the ListBox we set the IsSynchronizedWithCurrentItem property to true. The associated view model is injected into the constructor as the code in listing 6.25 shows.

Listing 6.25 – *Injecting the view-model into the customer list view*
```csharp
public CustomerListView(CustomerListViewModel vm)
{
    InitializeComponent();
    DataContext = vm;
}
```

Add the class definition presented in listing 6.26 to the CustomersModule project. This represents the view-model that is injected into the view constructor.

Listing 6.26 – *The CustomerListViewModel view-model definition*
```csharp
public class CustomerListViewModel:NotificationObject
{
    private ICustomerService custService;
    private IEventAggregator eventAggregator;
    public CustomerListViewModel(ICustomerService custService,
        IEventAggregator eventAggregator)
    {
        this.eventAggregator = eventAggregator;
        this.custService = custService;
    }
    private ICollectionView customers;
    public ICollectionView Customers
    {
        get {
            if (customers == null)
                InitCustomers();
            return customers;
        }
    }
    private void InitCustomers()
    {
        var data = custService.GetCustomers();
        customers = CollectionViewSource.GetDefaultView(data);
        customers.CurrentChanged += customers_CurrentChanged;
        RaisePropertyChanged("Customers");
```

```
    }
    void customers_CurrentChanged(object sender, EventArgs e)
    {
        Customer cust = customers.CurrentItem as Customer;
        if (cust == null)
            eventAggregator.GetEvent<CustomerSelectedEvent>()
                .Publish(null);
        else
            eventAggregator.GetEvent<CustomerSelectedEvent>()
                .Publish(cust.Id);
    }
}
```

We inject the customer service and the event aggregator into the constructor. When the customer collection is read for the first time we retrieve the customer list and build the ICollectionView that is bound to the list box. We also subscribe to the CurrentChanged event in order to keep track of the currently selected customer. When a new customer is selected, we publish the CustomerSelectedEvent event and pass it the id of the current item. This event is a CompositePresentationEvent that is used to communicate between view-models in a loosely coupled fashion. Add the following event definition to the Infrastructure project.

```
public class CustomerSelectedEvent:CompositePresentationEvent<int?>
{ }
```

The last thing we need to do in order to display the CustomerListView is to add it to the CustomersRegion. We do this using view discovery. Add the following code at the end of the CustomerModule.Initialize method.

```
regionManager.RegisterViewWithRegion("CustomersRegion", typeof(CustomerListView));
```

Displaying the customer details

Add a new user control to the CustomersModule project and name it CustomerDetailsView. The XAML shown in listing 6.27 presents this view's content.

Listing 6.27 – *The customer details view definition*
```
<Grid.RowDefinitions>
    <RowDefinition Height="auto"/>
    <RowDefinition/>
</Grid.RowDefinitions>
<Grid>
    <Grid.ColumnDefinitions>
        <ColumnDefinition Width="auto"/>
        <ColumnDefinition/>
    </Grid.ColumnDefinitions>
    <Grid.RowDefinitions>
        <RowDefinition Height="auto"/>
        <RowDefinition Height="auto"/>
        <RowDefinition Height="auto"/>
        <RowDefinition Height="auto"/>
```

```xml
    </Grid.RowDefinitions>
    <TextBlock Text="First Name" />
    <TextBox Text="{Binding Customer.FirstName, Mode=OneWay}" Grid.Column="1"/>
    <TextBlock Text="Last Name" Grid.Row="1"/>
    <TextBox Text="{Binding Customer.LastName, Mode=OneWay}"
        Grid.Column="1" Grid.Row="1"/>
    <TextBlock Text="Email" Grid.Row="2" />
    <TextBox Text="{Binding Customer.Email, Mode=OneWay}"
        Grid.Column="1" Grid.Row="2"/>
    <TextBlock Text="Phone" Grid.Row="3" />
    <TextBox Text="{Binding Customer.Phone, Mode=OneWay}"
        Grid.Column="1" Grid.Row="3"/>
</Grid>
<DataGrid IsReadOnly="True" Grid.Row="1" ItemsSource="{Binding Orders}"
        AutoGenerateColumns="False">
    <DataGrid.Columns>
        <DataGridTextColumn Header="Order Data" Binding="{Binding OrderDate}"/>
        <DataGridTextColumn Header="Shipping Cost" Binding="{Binding ShippingCost}"/>
        <DataGridTextColumn Header="Address" Binding="{Binding ShipAddress}"/>
        <DataGridTextColumn Header="Region" Binding="{Binding ShipRegion}"/>
    </DataGrid.Columns>
</DataGrid>
```

The corresponding view-model is injected in the view's constructor. This can be seen in listing 6.28.

Listing 6.28 - *Injecting the view-model into the customer details view*
```csharp
public CustomerDetailsView(CustomerDetailsViewModel vm)
{
    InitializeComponent();
    DataContext = vm;
}
```

Add the class definition presented in listing 6.29 to the CustomersModule project.

Listing 6.29 – *The CustomerDetailsViewModel view-model definition*
```csharp
public class CustomerDetailsViewModel:NotificationObject
{
    private ICustomerService custService;
    private Customer customer;
    private List<Order> orders;
    public CustomerDetailsViewModel(ICustomerService custService,
        IEventAggregator eventAggregator)
    {
        this.custService = custService;
        eventAggregator.GetEvent<CustomerSelectedEvent>()
            .Subscribe(OnCustomerSelected);
    }
    public void OnCustomerSelected(int? custId)
    {
        if (!custId.HasValue) return;
```

```csharp
        Customer = custService.GetCustomer(custId.Value);
        Orders = custService.GetCustomerOrders(custId.Value);
    }
    public Customer Customer
    {
        get { return customer; }
        private set
        {
            if (customer == value) return;
            customer = value;
            RaisePropertyChanged("Customer");
        }
    }
    public List<Order> Orders
    {
        get { return orders; }
        private set
        {
            if (orders == value) return;
            orders = value;
            RaisePropertyChanged("Orders");
        }
    }
}
```

The view-model uses the event aggregator to subscribe to the CustomerSelectedEvent event. When a new customer is selected, the view model uses the injected customer service to retrieve the customer details and orders. The last thing we need to do is to add this view to the CustomerDetailsRegion region. We do this with view discovery. Add the following line at the end of the module's Initialize method.

```csharp
regionManager.RegisterViewWithRegion("CustomerDetailsRegion",
    typeof(CustomerDetailsView));
```

The application is ready at this point. The application uses both view discovery (for regions that have static content) and view injection (for regions whose content changes frequently). Running it you should see something similar to what is shown in figure 6.7.

RegionContext

Every region exposes a Context property that can be used to share data between the views inside the region. In XAML we can set this context by using the RegionManager.RegionContext attached property. One example of when the RegionContext property might be used is in a master-details scenario. In this case we can use the RegionContext to supply the currently selected item to the views contained in the details region. The views can then use this data to show different aspects of the selected entity.

The RegionContext property can represent either a simple value, like an id, or it can be a complex object. It can be set normally or by using data binding. The RegionContext can be set either in XAML or in code. Listing 6.30 shows how to set the RegionContext property in XAML.

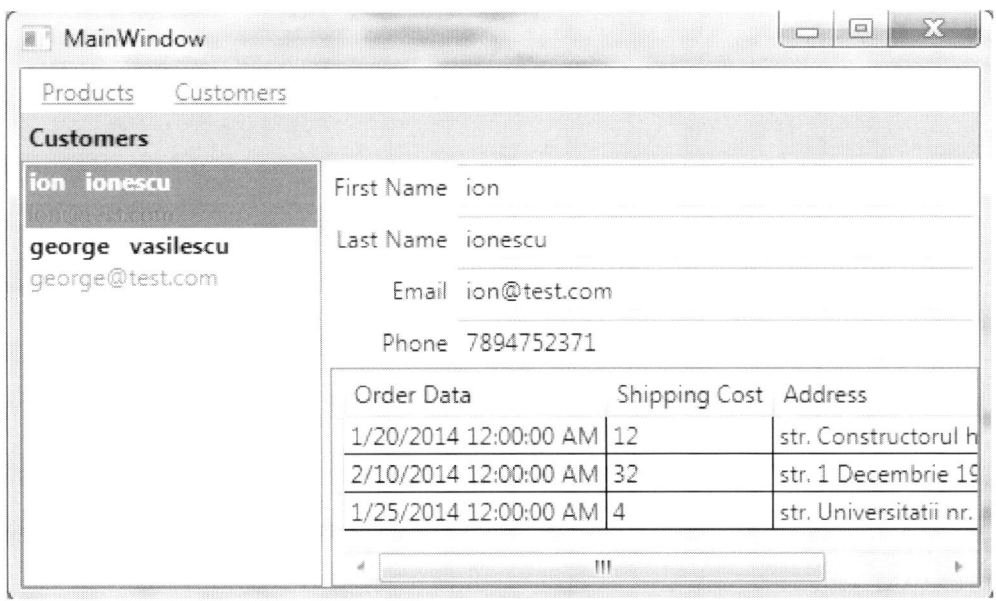

Figure 6.7 – *The customers view displayed in the application UI*

Listing 6.30 – *Setting the region's Context property in XAML*
```xml
<ContentControl p:RegionManager.RegionContext="{Binding Customer}"
                p:RegionManager.RegionName="DetailsRegion"/>
```

You can see that in the previous example the RegionContext is set on the control that hosts the region. One way to set the RegionContext in code is to get a reference to the region we want to use and set a value for its Context property. The code presented in listing 6.31 shows an example.

Listing 6.31 – *Setting the region's Context property in code*
```csharp
IRegion region = regionManager.Regions["DetailsRegion"];
region.Context = Customer;
```

The RegionContext can be read inside a view by using the GetObservableContext static method in the RegionContext class. This method accepts a single argument of type DependencyObject. This argument is the view for which we want to retrieve the context. Since the RegionContext attached property is set for a view inside a region, this view needs to derive from DependencyObject. The code presented in listing 6.32 shows how to retrieve the RegionContext from within a view.

Listing 6.32 – *Retrieving the Context property from a view inside the region*
```csharp
ObservableObject<object> context = RegionContext.GetObservableContext(this);
Customer customer = context.Value as Customer;
```

The view can be either a visual element that indirectly derives from DependencyObject or it can be a view-model that is displayed by a data template. In this case the view-model needs to derive from DependencyObject.

The RegionContext can also be modified in the views by assigning a value to the ObservableObject.Value property. Multiple views can remain synchronized by subscribing to the change event that is triggered when the RegionContext changes. The code presented in listing 6.33 shows how this is done. When the context changes we can now forward the value to the view-model.

Listing 6.33 – *Monitoring region Context changes*
```
ObservableObject<object> context = RegionContext.GetObservableContext(this);
context.PropertyChanged += (s, e) => {
    //region context changed
};
```

Using a RegionContext in the sample application

In order to show how the RegionContext can be used, we will modify the customer application we have built so far. We need to change the CustomerDetailsRegion region to be hosted in a TabControl in order to be able to display multiple views at the same time. We also need to update the region's Context property every time the selected customer changes. In this way, we can refresh the customer details view and customer orders view to display the correct data. We will replace the entire CustomerDetailsView view with two new views. These views will display the customer details and the customer orders respectively.

The first step we need to take is to change the type of control that will host our CustomerDetailsRegion region. Replace the content of the CustomersView view to match the content shown in listing 6.34.

Listing 6.34 – *The CustomersView view definition*
```
<ContentControl HorizontalContentAlignment="Stretch"
        VerticalContentAlignment="Stretch"
        p:RegionManager.RegionName="CustomersRegion"/>
<GridSplitter Grid.Column="1" HorizontalAlignment="Stretch"
        VerticalAlignment="Stretch" Width="4"/>
<TabControl HorizontalContentAlignment="Stretch"
        VerticalContentAlignment="Stretch"
        p:RegionManager.RegionName="CustomerDetailsRegion" Grid.Column="2"
        p:RegionManager.RegionContext="{Binding CustomerId}">
    <TabControl.ItemContainerStyle>
        <Style TargetType="TabItem">
            <Setter Property="Header" Value="{Binding DataContext.Title}"/>
        </Style>
    </TabControl.ItemContainerStyle>
</TabControl>
```

You can see that only the CustomerDetailsRegion region host control has changed to a TabControl. In order to display the item headers we apply a style for the item container. The headers will display the value of a Title property that will be exposed in the view-models.

The easiest way to update the region context is to subscribe to the CustomerSelectedEvent and set the context every time a new customer is selected. We can do this in the CustomersViewModel view-model. This is the view-model for the CustomersView view. Add the class definition shown in listing 6.35 to the CustomersModule project.

Listing 6.35 – *The CustomersViewModel view-model definition*
```
public class CustomersViewModel:NotificationObject
{
    public CustomersViewModel(IEventAggregator eventAggregator)
    {
        eventAggregator.GetEvent<CustomerSelectedEvent>()
            .Subscribe(OnCustomerSelected, ThreadOption.UIThread);
    }
    private int? custId;
    public int? CustomerId {
        get { return custId; }
        private set
        {
            if (custId == value) return;
            custId = value;
            RaisePropertyChanged("CustomerId");
        }
    }
    public void OnCustomerSelected(int? custId)
    { CustomerId = custId; }
}
```

This view-model exposes a CustomerId property that is data bound to the region context of the CustomerDetailsRegion region. This view-model will be injected into the view's constructor as listing 6.36 shows.

Listing 6.36 – *Injecting the view-model into the view*
```
public CustomersView(CustomersViewModel vm)
{
    InitializeComponent();
    DataContext = vm;
}
```

The next step is to register our views with the CustomerDetailsRegion region. We do this using view discovery since these views will remain in the region for the entire application lifetime. Modify the module initialization code for the CustomersModule module as shown in listing 6.37.

Listing 6.37 – *Registering the new views with the customer details region*
```
public void Initialize()
{
    //...
    //regionManager.RegisterViewWithRegion("CustomerDetailsRegion",
    //typeof(CustomerDetailsView));
    regionManager.RegisterViewWithRegion("CustomerDetailsRegion",
        typeof(DetailsView));
    regionManager.RegisterViewWithRegion("CustomerDetailsRegion",
        typeof(OrdersView));
}
```

You can see that we registered 2 new views with the CustomerDetailsRegion region. These views don't exist yet but we will create them shortly. The DetailsView view will display the customer details while the OrdersView view will display the customer orders. Also, the previous view registration has been commented out.

Creating the new views

The new views are easily created by copying the XAML from the previous CustomerDetailsView view. Add a new user control to the CustomersModule and name it DetailsView. This view can be seen in figure 6.8.

Figure 6.8 – *The customer details view*

You can clearly see that this view contains the customer details part from the previous view. Even the bindings were maintained. Add the class definition presented in listing 6.38 to the CustomersModule project in order to create the view's view-model.

Listing 6.38 – *The DetailsViewModel view-model definition*
```
public class DetailsViewModel:NotificationObject
{
    public string Title { get { return "Customer Details"; } }
    private ICustomerService custService;
    private Customer customer;
    public DetailsViewModel(ICustomerService custService)
    {
        this.custService = custService;
    }
    public Customer Customer
    {
        get { return customer; }
        private set
        {
            if (customer == value) return;
            customer = value;
            RaisePropertyChanged("Customer");
        }
    }
    public void SetRegionContext(object regionContext)
    {
        int? context = regionContext as int?;
        if (!context.HasValue)
```

```
            Customer = null;
        else
            Customer = custService.GetCustomer(context.Value);
    }
}
```

The view-model uses the customer service to retrieve the customer details. The details will be stored in the Customer property and will be updated every time we change the region context by calling the SetRegionContext method. This method will be called from the view as you will shortly see. Add the code presented in listing 6.39 to the view's code behind.

Listing 6.39 – *Listening to context changes and forwarding the new value to the view-model*
```
public DetailsView(DetailsViewModel vm)
{
    InitializeComponent();
    DataContext = vm;
    var context=RegionContext.GetObservableContext(this);
    context.PropertyChanged += (s, e) => {
        vm.SetRegionContext(context.Value);
    };
}
```

After the view-model is injected into the constructor and set as the view's data context we get a reference to the view's region context by calling GetObservableContext method. In order to synchronize the view every time the region context changes we subscribe to the PropertyChanged event. In this event we call the view-model's SetRegionContext method and pass the region context as the method argument.

We follow the same steps to display the customer orders. Add a new user control to the CustomersModule project and name it OrdersView. The XAML shown in listing 6.40 presents the view's content.

Listing 6.40 – *The OrdersView view definition*
```
<DataGrid IsReadOnly="True" ItemsSource="{Binding Orders}"
        AutoGenerateColumns="False">
    <DataGrid.Columns>
        <DataGridTextColumn Header="Order Data" Binding="{Binding OrderDate}"/>
        <DataGridTextColumn Header="Shipping Cost" Binding="{Binding ShippingCost}"/>
        <DataGridTextColumn Header="Address" Binding="{Binding ShipAddress}"/>
        <DataGridTextColumn Header="Region" Binding="{Binding ShipRegion}"/>
    </DataGrid.Columns>
</DataGrid>
```

Add the class definition presented in listing 6.41 to create the view's view-model.

Listing 6.41 – *The OrdersViewModel view-model definition*
```
public class OrdersViewModel:NotificationObject
{
    public string Title { get { return "Orders"; } }
    private List<Order> orders;
```

```
    private ICustomerService custService;
    public OrdersViewModel(ICustomerService custService)
    {
        this.custService = custService;
    }
    public List<Order> Orders
    {
        get { return orders; }
        private set
        {
            if (orders == value) return;
            orders = value;
            RaisePropertyChanged("Orders");
        }
    }
    public void SetRegionContext(object regionContext)
    {
        int? context = regionContext as int?;
        if (!context.HasValue)
            Orders = new List<Order>();
        else
            Orders = custService.GetCustomerOrders(context.Value);
    }
}
```

You can see that the Orders collection is updated every time we call the SetRegionContext method. Listing 6.42 presents the view's code-behind. You can see that we subscribe to the PropertyChanged event on the region context and when the context changes we call the view-model's SetRegionContext property.

Listing 6.42 – *Listening to Context changes and forwarding the new value to the view-model*
```
public OrdersView(OrdersViewModel vm)
{
    InitializeComponent();
    DataContext = vm;
    var context = RegionContext.GetObservableContext(this);
    context.PropertyChanged += (s, e) =>
    {
        vm.SetRegionContext(context.Value);
    };
}
```

The application is ready to run at this point and it looks exactly like in the first image in this chapter. There is only one problem with this implementation: we have code in the code behind. It is true that this is infrastructure code but we can do better.

Custom Region Behaviors
In order to access the RegionContext from a view that does not derive from DependencyObject we can write a custom RegionBehavior. This RegionBehavior will monitor the changes in the RegionContext and will forward that RegionContext to all views that do not derive from

DependencyObject. In order for this to happen the views will implement a custom interface. We will use this interface inside the region behavior to set the RegionContext value on the corresponding views.

We can implement a custom region behavior in 2 ways: implement the IRegionBehavior interface or derive from the RegionBehavior base class. RegionBehavior is an abstract base class that implements the IRegionBehavior interface. The class exposes a virtual OnAttach method that we can use in our derived behavior classes. This is the approach we will use.

In order to set the RegionContext on a view-model we'll use the custom interface presented in listing 6.43.

Listing 6.43 – *The IRegionContextAware interface definition*
```
public interface IRegionContextAware
{
    void SetRegionContext(object context);
}
```

This interface will expose a single method that will be used to set the region context into the view-model. Add this interface definition to the Infrastructure project. This is necessary because the interface is accessed both by the application modules and the Shell. Add the class definition shown in listing 6.44 to the Shell project.

Listing 6.44 – *Defining the custom region behavior*
```
public class RCForwardingRegionBehavior:RegionBehavior
{
    protected override void OnAttach()
    {
        throw new NotImplementedException();
    }
}
```

You can see that we provided a method override for the OnAttach virtual method that is defined in the base RegionBehavior class. What we want to do in this method is to subscribe to the region's PropertyChanged event. This event will be triggered every time a region property changes. Add the implementation for the OnAttach method as shown in listing 6.45.

Listing 6.45 – *Subscribing to the region's PropertyChanged event*
```
protected override void OnAttach()
{
    Region.PropertyChanged += Region_PropertyChanged;
}
```

Add the implementation for the Region_PropertyChanged event handler as shown in listing 6.46.

Listing 6.46 – *Handle region property changes*
```
private void Region_PropertyChanged(object sender, PropertyChangedEventArgs e)
{
    if (e.PropertyName != "Context") return;
```

```
//context has changed. forward context to view-models
foreach (var view in Region.Views)
{
    if (!(view is DependencyObject) && view is IRegionContextAware)
    {
        IRegionContextAware rca = view as IRegionContextAware;
        rca.SetRegionContext(Region.Context);
    }
    else if (view is FrameworkElement)
    {
        FrameworkElement el=view as FrameworkElement;
        IRegionContextAware rca = el.DataContext as IRegionContextAware;
        if (rca != null)
            rca.SetRegionContext(Region.Context);
    }
}
}
```

In the event handler we check to see what property has changed. If the property that changed is not the Context property we do nothing. If the Context property changed, we iterate over all the views in the region and look for views that implement the IRegionContextAware interface. When we find such a view, we forward the region context by using the Region.Context property. We also skip over views that derive from DependencyObject since we can already retrieve the context for these views by using the RegionContext.GetObservableContext method.

You can see that we also check the DataContext property to determine if the view-model implements the interface. This allows us to retrieve the region context even if we use a view-first approach to composing the views and view-models.

After we defined the region behavior we need to register it in the bootstrapper. We do this by overriding the ConfigureDefaultRegionBehaviors method. Add the method definition presented in listing 6.47 to override this method.

Listing 6.47 – *Registering the custom region behavior at a global level*
```
protected override IRegionBehaviorFactory ConfigureDefaultRegionBehaviors()
{
    var res = base.ConfigureDefaultRegionBehaviors();
    res.AddIfMissing("RegionContextForwarding", typeof(RCForwardingRegionBehavior));
    return res;
}
```

You can see that this method returns an IRegionBehaviorFactory implementation. For this we call the base implementation and keep a reference to the result. We then add our behavior and return the factory instance.

We need to add our custom behavior to this factory if we want our behavior to apply to all regions. If we want this behavior to apply to a single region we can directly add it to that region by using the code shown in listing 6.48.

Listing 6.48 – *Register the custom region behavior at a local level*
```
var behavior = new RCForwardingRegionBehavior();
```

```
container.Resolve<IRegionManager>()
        .Regions["CustomerDetailsRegion"].Behaviors
        .Add("RegionContextForwarding", behavior);
```

In this case we need to make sure to add these lines after the CustomerDetailsRegion region has been registered with the region manager. This can be done immediately after the CustomersView view has been added to the MainRegion region. Also, the behavior needs to be implemented in the corresponding module.

The next thing we need to do is to remove the PropertyChanged handlers from the view code-behind files. This can be seen in listing 6.49.

Listing 6.49 – *Stop listening for property changes*
```
public DetailsView(DetailsViewModel vm)
{
    InitializeComponent();
    DataContext = vm;
}
public OrdersView(OrdersViewModel vm)
{
    InitializeComponent();
    DataContext = vm;
}
```

At the end, we need to implement the IRegionContextAware interface on the 2 view-models: DetailsViewModel and OrdersViewModel. We only need to change the class declaration since the SetRegionContext method already exists in the view-models. This can be seen in listing 6.50.

Listing 6.50 – *Implementing the IRegionContextAware interface*
```
public class OrdersViewModel:NotificationObject, IRegionContextAware
{...}
public class DetailsViewModel:NotificationObject, IRegionContextAware
{...}
```

6.5 Summary

This chapter talked about regions. Regions are named placeholders that can contain zero or more views. Regions can contain any type of content. Regions decouple the views that need to be displayed from the location where they are displayed. Modules can add their own views to the application without knowing where they will be shown. Views can be added to a region in 2 ways.

View discovery is the process by which views are registered with a particular region. When that region is displayed it searches for all registered views and populates itself, thus displaying the views. View discovery is used when the region views do not change over the lifetime of the application.

View injection is the process by which views are added to a region at runtime by using code. View injection can be used in navigation scenarios, where a region's views change a lot during the application's usage. Another reason for using view injection is if we want to display multiple instances of the same view but with different parameters. View injection also allows us to delete the views inside a region.Insert chapter six text here.

CHAPTER 7: REGION NAVIGATION

When the user interacts with an application its interface changes to reflect the task the user is currently performing. The interface can change significantly over time as the user finishes the various tasks. The process by which these UI changes are managed is called navigation. There are 2 types of navigation that PRISM recognizes: state-based navigation and view-based navigation. The rest of this chapter will talk, in detail, about these types of navigation.

7.1 State-based navigation

In this type of navigation the view is updated either by property changes in the view-model or by interacting with the view itself. State-based navigation does not replace one view with another, but rather updates the existing view. Two examples that can be given are: presenting view availability via a busy indicator and presenting different views for the same data.

Presenting a busy indicator that temporarily prevents access to the UI can be implemented by an IsBusy Boolean property in the view-model. Before starting the long running operation we set the IsBusy property to true. After the operation completes, either successfully or with an error, we set the IsBusy property to false. This can be seen in listing 7.1.

Listing 7.1 – *Setting the busy state while saving*
```
private bool isBusy;
public bool IsBusy
{
    get { return isBusy; }
    set
    {
        if (isBusy == value) return;
        isBusy = value;
        RaisePropertyChanged("IsBusy");
    }
}
private void OnSave()
{
    IsBusy = true;
```

```
    peopleService.Save(ex => {
        Deployment.Current.Dispatcher.BeginInvoke(() => {
            IsBusy = false;
            //handle exception
        });
    });
}
```

You need to make sure you modify the IsBusy property on the UI thread since this will eventually update a UI element. On the UI side we bind some piece of UI to this IsBusy property. The target of the binding can be the Visibility property of a Border element. In order to convert the Boolean value to a Visibility value we can use a value converter. This can be seen in listing 7.2.

Listing 7.2 – *The busy indicator code*
```
<Border Background="#33000000"
    Visibility="{Binding IsBusy, Converter={StaticResource conv}}">
    <StackPanel Background="White" HorizontalAlignment="Center"
        VerticalAlignment="Center">
        <TextBlock Text="Working..." HorizontalAlignment="Center" Margin="5"/>
        <ProgressBar IsIndeterminate="{Binding IsBusy}" Width="100"
            Height="15" Margin="5"/>
    </StackPanel>
</Border>
```

Another option will be to expose a Visibility property in the view-model since this can be tested as well. This property can work in conjunction with the IsBusy property or it can be used on its own. When the long running operation is started we set the property to Visible. When the operation is completed, we set the property to Collapsed. This way we have a minimum number of properties to handle the busy state. Figure 7.1 presents how the interface will look when the IsBusy flag is set to true.

Figure 7.1 – *Displaying the busy indicator*

In Silverlight we can use the BusyIndicator control from the Silverlight Toolkit. This is a content control that exposes an IsBusy Boolean property. We can directly bind our view-model IsBusy property to the control's IsBusy property as listing 7.3 shows.

Listing 7.3 – *Using the Silverlight BusyIndicator control*
```
<toolkit:BusyIndicator IsBusy="{Binding IsBusy}" BusyContent="Working..."
```

```
    BorderBrush="#FF4E80C4" Background="#FFECECEF" BorderThickness="2">
...
</toolkit:BusyIndicator>
```

State based navigation can also be implemented, in Silverlight, by using the DataStateBehavior behavior. This behavior works in conjunction with the VisualStateManager. When we use this behavior we also need to define the visual states of the UI element we wish to change. The DataStateBehavior behavior can change between 2 states: TrueState and FalseState based on the value of the specified binding. The code in listing 7.4 shows how to use the behavior.

Listing 7.4 – *Using the DataStateBehavior to change visual states*
```
<i:Interaction.Behaviors>
    <ei:DataStateBehavior TrueState="BusyState" FalseState="IdleState"
        Binding="{Binding IsBusy}" Value="true"/>
</i:Interaction.Behaviors>
```

The DataStateBehavior can be found in the Microsoft.Expression.Interactions.dll assembly so be sure to add a reference to this assembly as well as to the namespace prefix, before using the code above. In the code above, when the IsBusy property is true the behavior will change to the BusyState state. The VisualStateManager can then define the visual states, shown in listing 7.5, for the UI element we want to update.

Listing 7.5 – *Visual states to present the busy interface*
```
<VisualStateManager.VisualStateGroups>
    <VisualStateGroup x:Name="BusyStates">
        <VisualState x:Name="BusyState">
            <Storyboard>
              <ObjectAnimationUsingKeyFrames Storyboard.TargetProperty
                 ="(UIElement.Visibility)" Storyboard.TargetName="border">
                <DiscreteObjectKeyFrame KeyTime="0" Value="Visible"/>
              </ObjectAnimationUsingKeyFrames>
            </Storyboard>
        </VisualState>
        <VisualState x:Name="IdleState"/>
    </VisualStateGroup>
</VisualStateManager.VisualStateGroups>
```

7.2 View-based navigation

The second type of navigation that PRISM supports is view-based navigation or view-switching. This navigation scenario is represented by the addition or removal of elements from the visual tree. Examples can include changing the content of a ContentControl or adding or removing items to and from a TabControl or ItemsControl. Navigation is done inside regions and is very similar to browser navigation. The user can also move forwards or backwards in the navigation history by using a journal.

View-based navigation is made possible by the INavigateAsync interface which exposes the RequestNavigate method. This interface is implemented by both IRegionNavigationService and IRegion interfaces. Most of the time, navigation will be performed by calling the RequestNavigate method on the IRegionManager implementation. The method is exposed here through the use of extension methods. The actual navigation logic is delegated to the IRegionNavigationService implementation.

To present the PRISM support for view-based navigation we will build a sample application that manages a list of customers. When the user selects a customer, a details view is displayed that allows the user to modify the customer.

Creating the application

Create a new Silverlight application project and add the required PRISM assemblies. We will use Unity as a dependency injection container so you should add the Unity specific assembly references to the project. In order to support user interaction scenarios, make sure you also add the following interactivity assemblies: Microsoft.Practices.Prism.Interactivity.dll, System.Windows.Interactivity.dll and Microsoft.Expression.Interactions.dll.

The next step is to create the Bootstrapper. Add the class definition presented in listing 7.6 to the Silverlight project.

Listing 7.6 – *The application bootstrapper definition*
```
public class Bootstrapper:UnityBootstrapper
{
    protected override DependencyObject CreateShell()
    {
        return Container.Resolve<MainPage>();
    }
    protected override void InitializeShell()
    {
        MainPage view = Shell as MainPage;
        App.Current.RootVisual = view;
    }
}
```

The application Shell will be composed of 2 regions: the main region and the details region. The main region, on the left, will display a list of customers. The details region, on the right, will display customer details data. The user will have the possibility to display details about multiple customers at once. This is done by using a TabControl. Add the style presented in listing 7.7 as a resource to the Shell view.

Listing 7.7 – *TabItem style resource definition*
```
<UserControl.Resources>
    <Style TargetType="sdk:TabItem" x:Key="itemStyle">
        <Setter Property="Header" Value="{Binding DataContext}" />
        <Setter Property="HeaderTemplate">
            <Setter.Value>
                <DataTemplate>
                    <TextBlock MinWidth="50" Text="{Binding Id}"/>
                </DataTemplate>
            </Setter.Value>
        </Setter>
    </Style>
</UserControl.Resources>
```

This style will be applied to every TabItem in order to properly display the customer details. The Silverlight implementation of the TabControl control does not expose the ItemContainerStyle property that is used to define the style for every TabItem. In order to set this style we use the TabControlRegionAdapter.ItemContainerStlye attached property offered by PRISM. Add the XAML in listing 7.8 to the Shell view.

Listing 7.8 – *The Shell view XAML definition*
```xaml
<Grid x:Name="LayoutRoot" Background="White">
    <Grid.ColumnDefinitions>
        <ColumnDefinition Width="*"/>
        <ColumnDefinition Width="*"/>
    </Grid.ColumnDefinitions>
    <ContentControl Grid.Column="0"
        prism:RegionManager.RegionName="MainRegion"
        HorizontalContentAlignment="Stretch" VerticalContentAlignment="Stretch" />
    <sdk:TabControl Grid.Column="1"
        prism:RegionManager.RegionName="DetailsRegion"
        prism:TabControlRegionAdapter.ItemContainerStyle="{StaticResource itemStyle}"
        />
</Grid>
```

As you can see, the view is composed of 2 columns. On the left we have the main region that will display the customer list and on the right we have the details region. Don't forget to add the namespace prefix for the PRISM library. The prefix for the TabControl as well as the necessary assembly references will be added when you drag and drop the TabControl from the toolbox.

Creating the customer service

Customers will be provided by a dummy customer service. Add the Customer class definition presented in listing 7.9 to the Silverlight project.

Listing 7.9 – *The Customer class definition*
```csharp
public class Customer
{
    public int Id { get; set; }
    public string FirstName { get; set; }
    public string LastName { get; set; }
    public string Email { get; set; }
}
```

Add the service definition and implementation presented in listing 7.10 to the Silverlight project. Notice we are returning a copy of the customer from the GetCustomer method. This allows us to explicitly save the changes by calling a Save method. The original customer will remain unchanged. This implementation works for in memory storage. When using EF, for example, this doesn't apply since the EF DbContext will instantiate all entities it retrieves from the database.

Listing 7.10 – *The ICustomerService service interface and implementation*
```csharp
public interface ICustomerService
```

```csharp
{
    List<Customer> GetCustomers();
    Customer GetCustomer(int id);
}
public class CustomerService : ICustomerService
{
    private List<Customer> customers = new List<Customer>()
    {
        new Customer(){Id=1, FirstName="Ion", LastName="Ionescu",
          Email="ion@test.com"},
        new Customer(){Id=2, FirstName="George", LastName="Georgescu",
          Email="geo@test.com"},
        new Customer(){Id=3, FirstName="Paul", LastName="Marinescu",
          Email="paul@test.com"},
    };

    public List<Customer> GetCustomers() { return customers; }

    public Customer GetCustomer(int id)
    {
        var cust = customers.Where(p => p.Id == id).SingleOrDefault();
        if (cust != null)
            return new Customer() { Id = id, FirstName = cust.FirstName,
                LastName = cust.LastName, Email = cust.Email };
        return null;
    }
}
```

This service will be injected into the application view-models. In order for this to happen we need to register the service with the Unity container. Add the ConfigureContainer method override, presented in listing 7.11, to the Bootstrapper class.

Listing 7.11 – *Registering the customer service with the Unity container*
```csharp
protected override void ConfigureContainer()
{
    base.ConfigureContainer();
    Container.RegisterInstance<ICustomerService>(new CustomerService());
}
```

Add the code presented in listing 7.12 to the Application_Startup event handler in the App class in order to initialize the application.

Listing 7.12 – *The application start-up code*
```csharp
private void Application_Startup(object sender, StartupEventArgs e)
{
    new Bootstrapper().Run();
}
```

Creating the views and view-models
The next step is to add the views that will display the data. Create a new Silverlight user control and

name it CustomerListView. This will be the view that will display our customer list. Add the XAML in listing 7.13 to this view.

Listing 7.13 – *The CustomerListView XAML definition*
```xml
<sdk:DataGrid IsReadOnly="True" AutoGenerateColumns="False"
        ItemsSource="{Binding Customers}"
        SelectedItem="{Binding SelectedCustomer, Mode=TwoWay}">
    <sdk:DataGrid.Columns>
        <sdk:DataGridTextColumn Header="First Name" Binding="{Binding FirstName}"/>
        <sdk:DataGridTextColumn Header="Last Name" Binding="{Binding LastName}"/>
        <sdk:DataGridTextColumn Header="Email" Binding="{Binding Email}"/>
    </sdk:DataGrid.Columns>
</sdk:DataGrid>
```

Add another Silverlight user control to the project and name it CustomerDetailsView. This will be the view that will display our customer details. Add the XAML presented in listing 7.14 to this view.

Listing 7.14 – *The CustomerDetailsView XAML definition*
```xml
<StackPanel Margin="5">
    <TextBlock Text="First Name" Margin="2"/>
    <TextBox Text="{Binding FirstName, Mode=TwoWay}" Margin="2"/>
    <TextBlock Text="Last Name" Margin="2"/>
    <TextBox Text="{Binding LastName, Mode=TwoWay}" Margin="2"/>
    <TextBlock Text="Email" Margin="2"/>
    <TextBox Text="{Binding Email, Mode=TwoWay}" Margin="2"/>
</StackPanel>
```

Navigating to the parent view

In order to display our customer list view we have a few choices: view discovery, view injection and view navigation. What we will do in this application is to use the third option. After the Shell is initialized we will navigate to the CustomerListView in the MainRegion region. Modify the Bootstrapper InitializeShell method as in listing 7.15.

Listing 7.15 – *Initializing the application shell*
```csharp
protected override void InitializeShell()
{
    MainPage view = Shell as MainPage;
    App.Current.RootVisual = view;
    IRegionManager rm = Container.Resolve<IRegionManager>();
    rm.RequestNavigate("MainRegion", "CustomerListView");
}
```

You can see that we get a reference to the region manager and use the RequestNavigate method in order to navigate to the desired view. Calling the RequestNavigate method will have the effect of showing the CustomerListView in the ContentControl on the left side of the Shell view.

This overload of the RequestNavigate method accepts 2 arguments of type string. The first argument is the name of the region where navigation will take place. The second argument is the name of the contract that will be used to retrieve the view from the Unity container. Every view that is the source of a navigation operation needs to be registered with the container as a named registration. The contract name needs to match the name of the view in order to get the correct behavior. The source type of the mapping needs to be an object. Modify the ConfigureContainer override as shown in listing 7.16 in order to add the required mappings.

Listing 7.16 – *Registering the view mappings for navigation*
```
protected override void ConfigureContainer()
{
    base.ConfigureContainer();
    Container.RegisterInstance<ICustomerService>(new CustomerService());
    Container.RegisterType<object, CustomerListView>("CustomerListView");
    Container.RegisterType<object, CustomerDetailsView>("CustomerDetailsView");
}
```

Notice that we are registering a type. This allows the container to create a new view instance each time we navigate. Had we used the RegisterInstance method, to register the views, we would have gotten the same instance over and over again. In this case only a single customer would be shown. I will get into more detail with this when I talk about how we can integrate with the navigation process.

There is also a RequestNavigate extension method overload that accepts a delegate. This delegate accepts a NavigationResult instance as an argument and is called when the navigation is completed either successfully or with an error. The code in listing 7.17 shows such a method call.

Listing 7.17 – *Executing code after a navigation operation finishes*
```
IRegionManager rm = Container.Resolve<IRegionManager>();
rm.RequestNavigate("MainRegion", "CustomerListView", args => {
    if (args.Error != null)
    {
        Debug.WriteLine(string.Format("Navigation error: {0}", args.Error.Message));
        return;
    }
    if (args.Result.HasValue && args.Result.Value)
        Debug.WriteLine("navigated");
    else
        Debug.WriteLine("Navigation cancelled");
});
```

Showing the customer list

Running the application at this point will show an empty UI. We need to link some view-models with the existing views. We develop this application using the view-first approach where the registered URIs point to the views. This means view-models need to be injected into the views via constructor injection. This will be done at navigation time when the views to be navigated to will be resolved from the DI container. Change the CustomerListView and CustomerDetailsView constructors as listing 7.18 shows.

Listing 7.18 – *Injecting the view-models in to the views*
```
public CustomerListView(CustomerListViewModel vm)
```

```csharp
{
    InitializeComponent();
    DataContext = vm;
}
public CustomerDetailsView(CustomerDetailsViewModel vm)
{
    InitializeComponent();
    DataContext = vm;
}
```

Add the class definition shown in listing 7.19 to the Silverlight project. The Customers and SelectedCustomer properties are already bound to the DataGrid control in the view in order to display the customer list.

Listing 7.19 – *The customer list view-model definition*
```csharp
public class CustomerListViewModel:NotificationObject
{
    private List<Customer> customers;
    private Customer selCustomer;
    private IRegionManager regionManager;

    public CustomerListViewModel(ICustomerService custService,
        IRegionManager regionManager)
    {
        this.regionManager = regionManager;
        customers = custService.GetCustomers();
    }
    public Customer SelectedCustomer
    {
        get { return selCustomer; }
        set
        {
            if (selCustomer == value) return;
            selCustomer = value;
            RaisePropertyChanged("SelectedCustomer");
        }
    }
    public List<Customer> Customers
    {
        get { return customers; }
    }
}
```

Showing customer details

To display the customer details we need to navigate to a new view, but this time the navigation will be done in the DetailsRegion region. Modify the SelectedCustomer property setter as shown in listing 7.20.

Listing 7.20 – *Navigating to the customer details page*
```csharp
public Customer SelectedCustomer
```

```
{
    get { return selCustomer; }
    set
    {
        if (selCustomer == value) return;
        selCustomer = value;
        RaisePropertyChanged("SelectedCustomer");
        if (selCustomer != null)
        {
            var q = new UriQuery();
            q.Add("id", selCustomer.Id.ToString());
            regionManager.RequestNavigate("DetailsRegion",
                "CustomerDetailsView" + q.ToString());
        }
    }
}
```

When the selected customer changes we initiate the navigation in the DetailsRegion region. We do this with the region manager reference that got injected into the constructor. We use the RequestNavigate method again, but this time we specify the DetailsRegion region. The question is: how do we know which customer to show in the new view?

PRISM allows us to pass navigation arguments in a query string, just like web sites do. In order to build the query string more easily, PRISM provides us with the UriQuery class. This class is used just like a dictionary, allowing us to add key-value pairs that represent the navigation arguments and their values. The constructed query string is then appended to the contract name.

Participating in the navigation sequence

In order for the details view to be able to read the navigation parameters, it needs to participate in the navigation sequence. This can be done by implementing the INavigationAware interface. The interface definition can be seen in listing 7.21.

Listing 7.21 – *The INavigationAware interface definition*
```
public interface INavigationAware
{
    void OnNavigatedTo(NavigationContext navigationContext);
    bool IsNavigationTarget(NavigationContext navigationContext);
    void OnNavigatedFrom(NavigationContext navigationContext);
}
```

The INavigationAware interface defines 3 methods. OnNavigatedTo is called on the new view-model after navigating to the new view. OnNavigatedFrom is called on the old view-model when navigating away from the current view. IsNavigationTarget is called after OnNavigatedFrom in order to determine if there are any candidate views already displayed.

All 3 methods accept a parameter of type NavigationContext. Using this argument we can access the navigation URI, the navigation parameters as well as the navigation service. In order to display the correct customer details, we need to involve the CustomerDetailsViewModel view-model in the navigation process. Add the definition for the CustomerDetailsViewModel view-model class as shown in listing 7.22.

Listing 7.22 – *The customer details view-model*
```csharp
public class CustomerDetailsViewModel:NotificationObject, INavigationAware
{
    private Customer customer;
    private ICustomerService custService;
    public CustomerDetailsViewModel(ICustomerService custService)
    {
        this.custService = custService;
    }
    public bool IsNavigationTarget(NavigationContext navigationContext)
    {
        return false;
    }
    public void OnNavigatedFrom(NavigationContext navigationContext)
    { }
    public void OnNavigatedTo(NavigationContext navigationContext)
    { }
}
```

The IsNavigationTarget method always returns false. This means that new views will always be created during navigation. This has the effect of showing multiple views for the same customer. We will change this in the next section. What we want to do is determine the current customer, from the navigation parameters, and store it for use. Add a definition for the OnNavigatedTo method as shown in listing 7.23.

Listing 7.23 – *Getting the current customer when navigating to the view-model*
```csharp
public void OnNavigatedTo(NavigationContext navigationContext)
{
    int id;
    if (int.TryParse(navigationContext.Parameters["id"], out id))
    {
        //don't refresh the customer
        if (customer != null && customer.Id == id) return;
        customer = custService.GetCustomer(id);
        RaisePropertyChanged("FirstName", "LastName", "Email", "Id");
    }
}
```

Here we access the Parameters property of the navigationContext argument and parse the id that was supplied during navigation. We then use the customer service to retrieve the customer. The details view-model will wrap the customer properties in order to provide change notification events. Add the properties shown in listing 7.24 to the CustomerDetailViewModel class. The LastName and Email properties are implemented in a similar manner to the FirstName property.

Listing 7.24 – *Customer properties that provide change notification*
```csharp
public int Id { get { return customer == null ? 0 : customer.Id; } }
public string FirstName
{
    get { return customer == null ? "" : customer.FirstName; }
```

```
set
{
    if (customer == null || customer.FirstName == value) return;
    customer.FirstName = value;
    RaisePropertyChanged("FirstName");
}
}
```

Running the application at this point should allow us to select a customer and view its details. The application should look similar to figure 7.2. You can see that we are able to open multiple views to edit the same customer. This does not provide a consistent experience. Users would expect to just activate the view if they navigate to an already existing customer.

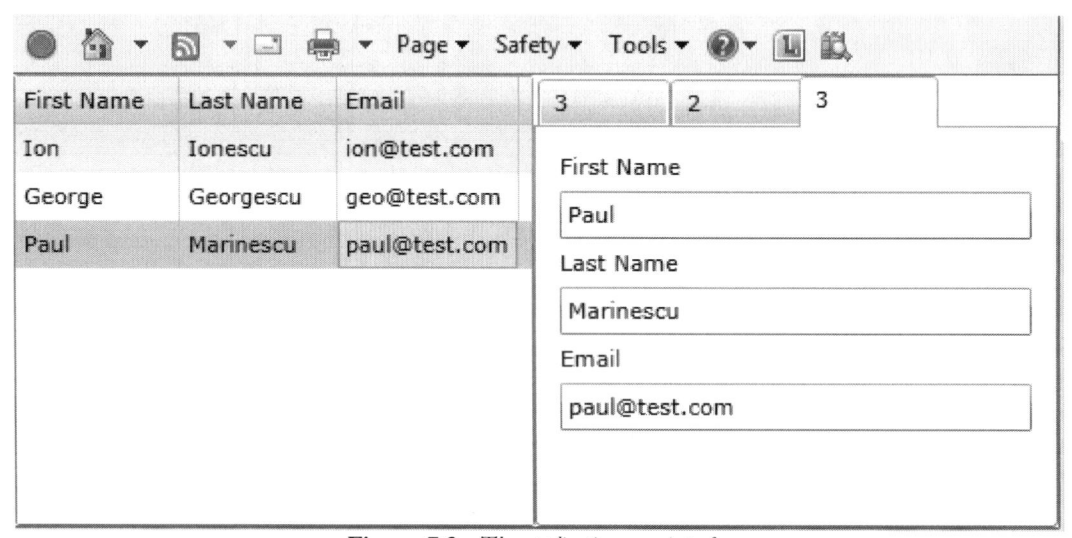

Figure 7.2 – *The application user interface*

Navigation targets

In order to fix our navigation problem we need to change the IsNavigationTarget implementation. What we want to do is check whether the current view-model contains the customer we just navigated to. If it does we specify that we want to reuse the view by returning true from the method. Otherwise we return false. Modify the IsNavigationTarget method to look like the implementation presented in listing 7.25.

Listing 7.25 - *Determining the navigation target*
```
public bool IsNavigationTarget(NavigationContext navigationContext)
{
    int id;
    if (int.TryParse(navigationContext.Parameters["id"], out id))
    {
        if (customer.Id == id)
            return true;
    }
```

```
        return false;
}
```

By using this implementation we can reuse an already opened view if the id parameter matches the customer id for the opened view. We can also go the other way and reuse a single view for all view-models. We do this by always returning true. The effect of this is that we get only one tab at any given time.

A similar thing happens if we register the views used for navigation as instances. I talked about this in a previous section. In this situation only a single view is presented regardless of the value returned from IsNavigationTarget. If the IsNavigationTarget method always returns false, we can't navigate to a new view because the single instance is always returned and OnNavigatedTo is only called once (for the first view inside the region). This also means only a single customer is ever shown. If the IsNavigationTarget method always returns true, we have a chance of correcting the contract registration error. This is because the OnNavigatedTo method will always be called, giving us the chance to properly reuse the single instance returned from the DI container.

The second problem can be considered a bug, but using a TabControl in the first situation doesn't really make sense. A content control would be more appropriate.

Controlling the view-model lifetime

Even if we can only see one view at a time in a particular region, the remaining, inactive, views are still held in that region. We can specify whether the inactive views should be removed or not by implementing the IRegionMemberLifetime interface. This interface has a single member, the read-only KeepAlive property, which specifies if the inactive view should be removed. Add the implementation of the IRegionMemberLifetime to the CustomerDetailsViewModel class as shown in listing 7.26.

Listing 7.26 – *Implementing IRegionMemberLifetime*
```
public bool KeepAlive
{
    get { return false; }
}
```

Tracking state changes

Before we talk about confirming navigation requests we need to add a few more features to the application. What we want to add is a feature that tells us whether the current customer has been modified and also allows us to save the changes. We can implement such a feature by adding a dirty flag and a save command. In the CustomerDetailsViewModel view-model add the properties shown in listing 7.27.

Listing 7.27 – *Detecting changes to the document*
```
private bool isDirty;
public string DirtyText { get { return isDirty ? "*" : ""; } }
protected bool IsDirty
{
    get { return isDirty; }
    set
    {
```

```
        if (isDirty == value) return;
        isDirty = value;
        RaisePropertyChanged("IsDirty");
        RaisePropertyChanged("DirtyText");
    }
}
```

The IsDirty property is set after each view-model property is modified (in the setter, before the property changed event is raised). This will also update the star that will be shown if the customer is dirty. In order to save the document we will add a command that will just set the dirty flag to false. Add the command in listing 7.28 to the view-model class.

Listing 7.28 – *Adding the save command to the details view model*
```
public CustomerDetailsViewModel(ICustomerService custService)
{
    this.custService = custService;
    saveCmd = new DelegateCommand(OnSave);
}
private DelegateCommand saveCmd;
public DelegateCommand SaveCommand { get { return saveCmd; } }
private void OnSave() { IsDirty = false; }
```

Modify the CustomerDetailsView view, as shown in listing 7.29, in order to bind the save command and update the corresponding view-model properties every time a text box value changes. We can use the PropertyChanged value for the UpdateSourceTrigger property in Silverlight 5. For earlier versions, PRISM provides the UpdateTextBindingOnPropertyChanged behavior. This behavior subscribes to the TextChanged event and updates the source of the binding whenever characters are added or removed. The class can be found in the PRISM Interactivity namespace.

Listing 7.29 – *Binding the customer details UI elements to the view-model properties*
```
<StackPanel Margin="5">
    <TextBlock Text="First Name" Margin="2"/>
    <TextBox Text="{Binding FirstName, Mode=TwoWay,
             UpdateSourceTrigger=PropertyChanged}" Margin="2"/>
    <TextBlock Text="Last Name" Margin="2"/>
    <TextBox Text="{Binding LastName, Mode=TwoWay,
             UpdateSourceTrigger=PropertyChanged}" Margin="2"/>
    <TextBlock Text="Email" Margin="2"/>
    <TextBox Text="{Binding Email, Mode=TwoWay,
             UpdateSourceTrigger=PropertyChanged}" Margin="2"/>
    <Button Content="Save" Command="{Binding SaveCommand}"
            HorizontalAlignment="Right" Margin="2"/>
</StackPanel>
```

In the Shell view, modify the TabItem HeaderTemplate data template, as shown in listing 7.30, to display the dirty state.

Listing 7.30 – *The new header template definition*
```
<DataTemplate>
```

```xml
    <StackPanel Orientation="Horizontal" MinWidth="50">
        <TextBlock Text="{Binding Id}"/>
        <TextBlock Text="{Binding DirtyText}"/>
    </StackPanel>
</DataTemplate>
```

Running the application at this point should allow us to edit the current customer and see the dirty flag. The application should look like the one in figure 7.3.

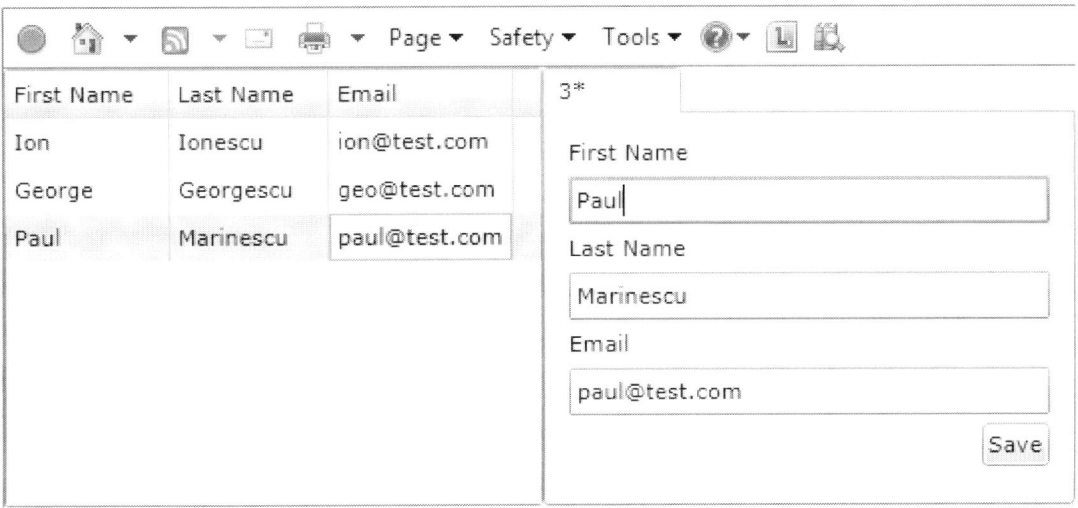

Figure 7.3 – *The main application UI after changing the header template*

Confirming navigation requests

Disposing of inactive views can present a problem if the user navigates away and there are pending changes. It would be nice if we could ask the user if he or she wishes to proceed with the navigation and lose the changes or to cancel the navigation. PRISM offers this option via the IConfirmNavigationRequest interface. This interface derives from INavigationAware and exposes a single method. The interface definition can be seen in listing 7.31.

Listing 7.31 – *The IConfirmNavigationRequest interface definition*
```csharp
public interface IConfirmNavigationRequest : INavigationAware
{
    void ConfirmNavigationRequest(NavigationContext navigationContext,
        Action<bool> continuationCallback);
}
```

The interface method is called before OnNavigatedFrom because the navigation may be cancelled. The continuationCallback delegate will be used to determine if the navigation should continue (passing true as the argument) or if the navigation should be cancelled (passing false as the argument). Before calling this callback the application can ask for the user's opinion. We can do this by using interaction request objects or an interaction service.

It is not necessary to call the continuation callback before the ConfirmNavigationRequest method finishes executing. We can call the callback at any time after we get the instance as long as we hold a reference to it and do not forget to call it.

The navigation process will be paused until this callback is called. If there is another navigation request before the callback is called, the current navigation is cancelled. Calling the callback after this point will have no effect since the previous navigation request no longer exists. If we always want to navigate to the new view we can directly call the continuationCallback delegate like listing 7.32 shows.

Listing 7.32 – *Always confirming the navigation request*
```
public void ConfirmNavigationRequest(NavigationContext navigationContext,
        Action<bool> continuationCallback)
{
    continuationCallback(true);
}
```

Add the implementation of the IConfirmNavigationRequest interface, shown in listing 7.33, to the CustomerDetailsViewModel view-model.

Listing 7.33 – *Asking the user to confirm the navigation request*
```
public void ConfirmNavigationRequest(NavigationContext navigationContext,
         Action<bool> continuationCallback)
{
    if (!IsDirty)
    {
        continuationCallback(true);
        return;
    }
    var c = new Confirmation() { Title = "Unsaved changes",
        Content = "Are you sure you want to navigate away?" };
        confReq.Raise(c, res => {
        if (c.Confirmed)
            continuationCallback(true);
        else
            continuationCallback(false);
    });
}
```

As you can see, we are using an interaction object to ask the user if he or she wants to navigate away, when they have pending changes. If the customer has not been modified we call the confirmation callback by passing true and return. If there are changes we are using the interaction request object. Add the property and initialization code shown in listing 7.34 to the CustomerDetailsViewModel class.

Listing 7.34 – *Defining the interaction request object used to confirm the navigation request*
```
public CustomerDetailsViewModel(ICustomerService custService)
{
    this.custService = custService;
    saveCmd = new DelegateCommand(OnSave);
    confReq = new InteractionRequest<Confirmation>();
```

```
}
private InteractionRequest<Confirmation> confReq;
public IInteractionRequest ConfirmRequest { get { return confReq; } }
```

In order to bind the interaction request object to the view, add the XAML presented in listing 7.35 to the CustomerDetailsView view. Also, do not forget to add the xml namespaces.

Listing 7.35 – *Binding the interaction request object*
```
xmlns:i="clr-
namespace:System.Windows.Interactivity;assembly=System.Windows.Interactivity"
xmlns:prism="http://www.codeplex.com/prism"

<UserControl.Resources>
    <DataTemplate x:Key="template">
        <TextBlock Text="{Binding}" />
    </DataTemplate>
</UserControl.Resources>
<i:Interaction.Triggers>
    <prism:InteractionRequestTrigger SourceObject="{Binding ConfirmRequest}">
        <prism:PopupChildWindowAction ContentTemplate="{StaticResource template}"/>
    </prism:InteractionRequestTrigger>
</i:Interaction.Triggers>
```

Even though we implemented the IConfirmNavigationRequest and INavigationAware interfaces on the view-models, these interfaces can also be implemented by the views. PRISM first checks the views for these interfaces. If they are not implemented by the view, PRISM then checks the instance that is passed as the view's data context.

Running the application at this point should allow you to stop the navigation if you have unsaved changes.

Using the navigation journal

PRISM navigation within a region is coordinated by a navigation service. This service is represented by the IRegionNavigationService interface. The interface definition can be seen in listing 7.36.

Listing 7.36 – *The region navigation service interface definition*
```
public interface IRegionNavigationService : INavigateAsync
{
    IRegion Region { get; set; }
    IRegionNavigationJournal Journal { get; }
    event EventHandler<RegionNavigationEventArgs> Navigating;
    event EventHandler<RegionNavigationEventArgs> Navigated;
    event EventHandler<RegionNavigationFailedEventArgs> NavigationFailed;
}
```

The service exposes a reference to the region that owns the service as well as a reference to the navigation journal. The 3 events are raised when the region is about to be navigated, when the region is navigated and when the navigation fails.

The navigation journal holds the entire navigation history for the particular region to which the navigation service belongs. The IRegionNavigationJournal definition can be seen in listing 7.37.

Listing 7.37 – *The navigation journal service interface definition*
```
public interface IRegionNavigationJournal
{
    bool CanGoBack { get; }
    bool CanGoForward { get; }

    IRegionNavigationJournalEntry CurrentEntry {get;}
    INavigateAsync NavigationTarget { get; set; }

    void GoBack();
    void GoForward();

    void RecordNavigation(IRegionNavigationJournalEntry entry);
    void Clear();
}
```

We can navigate forward or backward between the region views by using the GoForward and GoBack method respectively. We can also add journal entries as well as clear the navigation history. The GoBack method will not remove the views from the region; it will only navigate to the last entry in the journal. This can be more easily observed if we use the journal in a tabbed view. Using the GoForward and GoBack methods only allows us to change the current active view inside a region.

The steps made during journal navigation are identical to the ones made during the call to the RequestNavigate method. ConfirmNavigationRequest is called first, followed by OnNavigatedFrom. After this the navigation target is determined. The last call is made to OnNavigatedTo.

Using the navigation functions inside a region where the view-models return false from the IRegionmemberLifetime.KeepAlive property has the effect of recreating the view to which we are navigating and removing the current one (as expected).

Returning false from KeepAlive does not remove the journal entry from the navigation history after the view is removed. The same happens if we manipulate region views outside the navigation service. To see this in action lets implement some navigation in our sample application. Add the class definition shown in listing 7.38 to the Silverlight project.

Listing 7.38 – *Defining the shell view-model*
```
public class ShellViewModel
{
    private IRegionNavigationService navService;
    private DelegateCommand backCmd, fwdCmd;

    public ShellViewModel(IRegionManager regionManager)
    {
        navService = regionManager.Regions["DetailsRegion"].NavigationService;
        navService.Navigated += navService_Navigated;

        backCmd = new DelegateCommand(OnBack, CanGoBack);
        fwdCmd = new DelegateCommand(OnForward, CanGoForward);
    }
```

```csharp
    void navService_Navigated(object sender, RegionNavigationEventArgs e)
    {
        backCmd.RaiseCanExecuteChanged();
        fwdCmd.RaiseCanExecuteChanged();
    }

    public DelegateCommand BackCommand { get { return backCmd; } }
    public DelegateCommand ForwardCommand { get { return fwdCmd; } }

    private bool CanGoBack() { return navService.Journal.CanGoBack; }
    private void OnBack() { navService.Journal.GoBack(); }

    private bool CanGoForward() { return navService.Journal.CanGoForward; }
    private void OnForward() { navService.Journal.GoForward(); }
}
```

This is a simple view-model that exposes 2 commands for forward and backward navigation respectively. The view-model is injected with the IRegionManager service. We use this service to get the navigation service for the DetailsRegion region. We subscribe to the Navigated event in order to invalidate the 2 commands when appropriate. The commands' handlers simply delegate to the navigation journal implementation. Modify the Bootstrapper.InitializeShell method to link this view-model to the Shell view.

```csharp
view.DataContext = Container.Resolve<ShellViewModel>();
```

Modify the second column in the Shell view in order to link the 2 commands to buttons in the UI. This can be seen in listing 7.39.

Listing 7.39 – *Adding the navigation buttons to the shell view*
```xml
<Grid Grid.Column="1">
    <Grid.RowDefinitions>
        <RowDefinition Height="auto"/>
        <RowDefinition />
    </Grid.RowDefinitions>
    <StackPanel Orientation="Horizontal" Grid.Row="0">
        <Button Content="&lt;" Command="{Binding BackCommand}" Margin="2"/>
        <Button Content="&gt;" Command="{Binding ForwardCommand}" Margin="2"/>
    </StackPanel>
    <sdk:TabControl Grid.Row="1" prism:RegionManager.RegionName="DetailsRegion"
      prism:TabControlRegionAdapter.ItemContainerStyle="{StaticResource itemStyle}"
    />
</Grid>
```

View-model first development

The application example presented so far used a view-first approach. As the name implies the view is created first and then the view-model. Because we used a view-first approach the Unity registration contract names were the names of the views. Also the destination types in the mappings were the view types. The view-first approach makes it easy to track which view-model the view is showing. The disadvantage of using view-first is that the view-model tends to be linked to the view. This makes it difficult to use the same view to present multiple view models.

The view-model first approach is indicated when the views are represented as data templates. This approach allows for a better separation between the views and view-models. Even if the view is a UserControl you can make a data template that is applied automatically in order to link it to the view-model. The disadvantage of the view-model first approach is that it is more difficult to set up in Silverlight. It's easy in Silverlight 5 because of the automatic data template feature, but in earlier versions we need to use the DataTemplateSelector class offered by PRISM to automatically change a content control's appearance when its content changes.

To change the previous application to a view-model first approach we need to encapsulate the views in data templates. We also need to use the view-models in the type registrations. The rest of the code should remain unchanged.

Navigation with MEF

Navigation with MEF is done the same way. The INavigateAsync interace is involved here as well. Region navigation can be done by using an IRegion instance, an IRegionNavigationService instance or the IRegionManager extension methods just as with Unity. The only thing that differs from the Unity navigation is the way we register the types we use to navigate.

When registering the types with MEF we need to use a named contract. Also we need to specify that we want a non shared creation policy. The code in listing 7.40 presents the equivalent MEF type registrations that were used in the previous sample application.

Listing 7.40 *– Registering view types for navigation using MEF*
```
[Export("CustomerDetailsView")]
[PartCreationPolicy(CreationPolicy.NonShared)]
public partial class CustomerListView : UserControl
{
    [ImportingConstructor]
    public CustomerListView(CustomerListViewModel vm)
    {
        InitializeComponent();
        DataContext = vm;
    }
}
[Export("CustomerDetailsView")]
[PartCreationPolicy(CreationPolicy.NonShared)]
public partial class CustomerDetailsView : UserControl
{
    [ImportingConstructor]
    public CustomerDetailsView(CustomerDetailsViewModel vm)
    {
        InitializeComponent();
        DataContext = vm;
    }
}
```

Extending the navigation framework

The PRISM navigation feature uses the names of the views (or view-models) as the contract names for type registrations. Not using this convention doesn't seem to cause any problems if you do not want to navigate the existing views. The problem is that if we use a different name, the IsNavigationTarged method won't be called and existing views won't be reused.

One extensibility point offered by PRISM is the IRegionNavigationContentLoader interface. Implementations of this interface are used to load the content during navigation. The interface definition can be seen in listing 7.41.

Listing 7.41 – *The region navigation content loader interface definition*
```
public interface IRegionNavigationContentLoader
{
    object LoadContent(IRegion region, NavigationContext navigationContext);
}
```

The LoadContent method is used to retrieve the content to which the navigation request applies. If we are navigating to an existing view this method returns that view. If we are navigating to a new view, the method returns that new instance.

Extending PRISM by implementing this interface can be difficult. A more common approach would be to derive from the default content loader implementation. This class offers 3 virtual methods that can be overridden. The RegionNavigationContentLoader implementation exposes the methods shown in listing 7.42.

Listing 7.42 – *Implementing the navigation content loader interface*
```
public class RegionNavigationContentLoader : IRegionNavigationContentLoader
{
    public object LoadContent(IRegion region, NavigationContext navigationContext);
    protected virtual object
       CreateNewRegionItem(string candidateTargetContract){...};
    protected virtual string
       GetContractFromNavigationContext(NavigationContext navigationContext){...};
    protected virtual IEnumerable<object> GetCandidatesFromRegion(
       IRegion region, string candidateNavigationContract)
       {...};
}
```

The CreateNewRegionItem method uses the candidateTargetContract to resolve a named registration using the service locator. The resolved instance will be the new view to which we are about to navigate. This method is called by LoadContent if there is no existing view that can handle the navigation request. If we want to run additional code during this creation stage we can also override this method. After calling the base implementation we can add our custom code.

The GetContractFromNavigationContext method is used to determine the name of the type registration from the navigation URI. This method parses the navigation URI filtering out the query parameters returning the name of the type registration.

The GetCandidatesFromRegion method analyses the candidateNavigationContract parameter and returns all the views in the specified region whose names match the contract name.

The important thing to remember is that we are trying to define a new mapping between the contract name and the view type that gets returned. The easiest implementation would be to just override the GetContractFromNavigationContext method. We will define our mappings here. One possible implementation can be seen in listing 7.43.

Listing 7.43 – *Implementing a custom region content loader*
```
public class CustomRegionContentLoader:RegionNavigationContentLoader
{
    public CustomRegionContentLoader(IServiceLocator serviceLocator)
        :base(serviceLocator) { }
    protected override string
        GetContractFromNavigationContext(NavigationContext navigationContext)
    {
        var contract = base.GetContractFromNavigationContext(navigationContext);

        if(contract=="Details")
            return typeof(CustomerDetailsView).Name;
        else if(contract=="List")
            return typeof(CustomerListView).Name;

        return contract;
    }
}
```

To use this content loader we only need to register it with the bootstrapper. This should be done in the ConfigureContainer method before the base method call. The code in listing 7.44 presents an example.

Listing 7.44 – *Registering the region content loader with the container*
```
protected override void ConfigureContainer()
{
    RegisterTypeIfMissing(typeof(IRegionNavigationContentLoader),
            typeof(CustomRegionContentLoader), true);
    base.ConfigureContainer();
}
```

7.3 Summary

This chapter talked about the navigation features offered by the PRISM library. Navigation is the process that manages the UI changes inside the application. PRISM differentiates between 2 styles of navigation. Navigation that is accomplished by changing the state of various UI elements is named state-based navigation. Navigation that is accomplished by adding or removing elements from the visual tree is named view-based navigation.

State-based navigation is accomplished by hiding or showing UI elements. This operation can be done by binding UI element properties to a view-model property that affects the element's visibility. One other option is to use a DataStateBehavior behavior in conjunction with the VisualStateManager.

View-based navigation is supported in PRISM via the INavigateAsync interface. This allows us to add or remove views from a particular region. View-models or views can participate in the navigation process by implementing the INavigationAware interface. Implementing this interface also allows us to read navigation parameters. Confirming the navigation request can be done by implementing the IConfirmNavigationRequest interface.Insert chapter seven text here.

CHAPTER 8: DEPLOYING PRISM APPLICATIONS

In order to successfully deploy a PRISM application you need to plan for deployment early on in the design phase. The deployment strategy will be affected by the application modules (if any) and their packaging. Silverlight applications have different considerations, when it comes to deployment, compared to WPF applications. This is because they are hosted in different environments. Silverlight applications are easier to deploy in almost all situations. The sections that follow talk about deploying Silverlight and WPF applications in more detail.

8.1 Deploying Silverlight applications

Silverlight applications are deployed by using XAP files. The XAP file is the unit of deployment. These files are zip files that contain a manifest and all the application assemblies. To deploy a Silverlight application we need to copy the application XAP to a location on the web server. This location is usually the ClientBin folder of the web site that will expose the Silverlight application. After this we need to specify the path to the XAP file as the source argument of the object tag.

Silverlight application deployment can be done either by manually copying the XAP files to the server or automatically, in Visual Studio, by deploying the web application project containing the Silverlight application. The second option involves making sure that the Silverlight application is included in the web application's list of Silverlight applications as shown in figure 8.1.

You can add or remove Silverlight applications from a web application by opening the web application's property page and selecting the Silverlight Applications tab on the right side as figure 8.1 demonstrates.

For modular applications, modules can be packaged in different ways. If a module's content is to be presented at application startup, the module should probably be referenced by the Shell application in order to be downloaded at the same time. Also the module should be packaged in a Silverlight Class Library Project assembly.

If, on the other hand, the module's content is loaded after the main application has been downloaded, the module should be packaged in its own XAP file and placed in the same folder as the application Shell. This is done by implementing the module code in its own Silverlight application project. This project will then be added to the web application's Silverlight applications list.

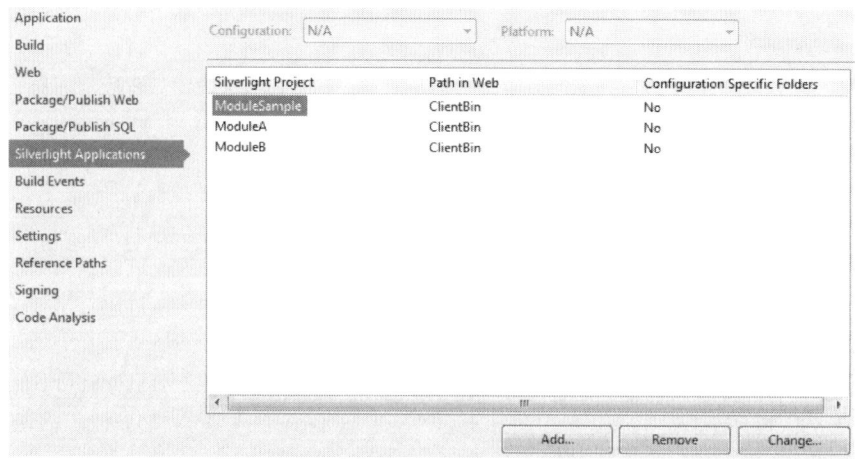

Figure 8.1 - The web application properties page

For out of browser deployments the modules should be packaged in the same XAP as the Shell application. When the Application.CheckAndDownloadUpdateAsync method is called only the main application XAP will be updated.

There is a problem when it comes to deploying modular Silverlight applications in which multiple modules and the Shell have references to the same shared assemblies (for example an infrastructure assembly, or the PRISM assemblies). In this case the shared assemblies are downloaded once for the Shell and once for each module that references them. This results in longer downloads and more bandwidth usage. In order to fix this problem we have a couple of options.

The first option is to set the CopyLocal property of the reference to the shared assembly to false in the properties window. This should be done on the module references only. There is no need to set the property to true here since the Shell has already downloaded the assemblies.

The second option is to use the Silverlight application library caching feature. This feature can be enabled for every Silverlight application by opening the properties window and checking the Reduce XAP size by using Application Library Caching option. When this option is checked the shared assemblies, that have the associated metadata files located correctly, will not be copied to the XAP file. Instead they will be placed in separate zip files that will be referenced by the XAP file.

Figure 8.2 presents a Silverlight application composed of 2 modules. Each module is packaged in its own XAP file. The library caching feature has not been activated for any of the 3 XAP files (modules and Shell). As a result the shared assemblies are present in each XAP file. When the modules are downloaded, the shared assemblies are downloaded as well.

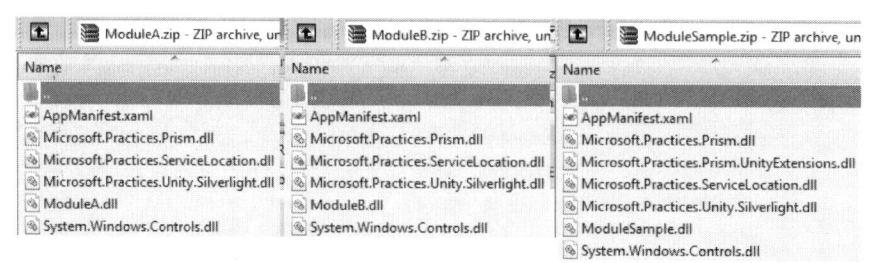

Figure 8.2 – Deployment structure for a Silverlight application that doesn't use assembly caching

The Silverlight assemblies for PRISM (as well as the other Silverlight assemblies) come with special metadata files (.extmap.xml) that allows them to be used with the assembly caching feature. Figure 8.3 presents the same application, but this time the assembly caching option is checked for all 3 Silverlight projects. Also the metadata files for the PRISM libraries have been copied to the assemblies' location since the assemblies weren't referenced from their install location. The other option is to reference the PRISM Silverlight assemblies from the install directory.

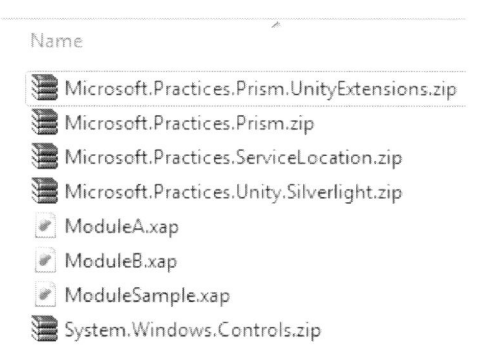

Figure 8.3 – *ClientBin folder contents for a Silverlight application that uses assembly caching*

Figure 8.3 presents the contents of the ClientBin folder in the web application. You can notice that the shared assemblies have been copied as zip files. Also, the modules no longer contain these files. This can be seen in figure 8.4.

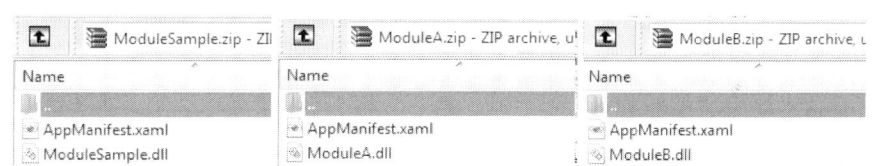

Figure 8.4 – *XAP contents for Silverlight applications that use assembly caching*

References to the shared assemblies are stored in the manifest file. Listing 8.1 presents the example for the ModuleA module.

Listing 8.1 – *Application manifest content for the ModuleA module.*
```
<Deployment
xmlns="http://schemas.microsoft.com/client/2007/deployment"
xmlns:x="http://schemas.microsoft.com/winfx/2006/xaml"
EntryPointAssembly="ModuleA" EntryPointType="ModuleA.App"
RuntimeVersion="5.0.61118.0">
  <Deployment.Parts>
    <AssemblyPart x:Name="ModuleA" Source="ModuleA.dll" />
  </Deployment.Parts>
  <Deployment.ExternalParts>
    <ExtensionPart Source="Microsoft.Practices.Prism.zip" />
    <ExtensionPart
        Source="Microsoft.Practices.ServiceLocation.zip" />
```

```xml
    <ExtensionPart
         Source="Microsoft.Practices.Unity.Silverlight.zip" />
    <ExtensionPart Source="System.Windows.Controls.zip" />
  </Deployment.ExternalParts>
</Deployment>
```

If you want to share your own assemblies all you need to do is supply the correct metadata file. This file has the same name as the assembly file you want to share. The extension is .extmap.xml. Listing 8.2 presents the contents of the metadata file for the Infrastructure.dll assembly. The file should be located in the same path as the assembly.

Listing 8.2 – *The contents of the .extmap.xml file for the Infrastructure.dll assembly*
```xml
<manifest>
  <assembly>
    <name>Infrastructure</name>
    <version>1.0.0.0</version>
    <publickeytoken>31bf3856ad364e35</publickeytoken>
    <relpath>Infrastructure.dll</relpath>
    <extension downloadUri="Infrastructure.zip"/>
  </assembly>
</manifest>
```

8.2 Deploying WPF applications

A WPF application is composed of an executable assembly and 0 or more class library assemblies. These class library assemblies can represent modules or shared assemblies. Additionally, an application can contain resource files that also need to be deployed.

We have the following options when deploying a WPF application: x-copy deployment, click once and windows installer. The x-copy deployment involves manually packaging and deploying the application. This process is error prone as the user might forget to copy some files or might not respect the correct folder structure. Usually a more automated solution is used to deploy WPF applications.

The automated options are: click once and windows installer. You can choose one of these options depending on your installation requirements. If you want to have a minimal footprint you can choose click once. If you want to install additional services with your application or if you want to modify the registry, you can choose to use an installer. The sections below present how to deploy PRISM applications using both techniques.

8.2.1 Deploying WPF PRISM applications with ClickOnce

You can publish a WPF application using ClickOnce by right clicking the Shell application and choosing the Publish option from the context menu. The ClickOnce wizard will guide you through the publish process. If you want to set up additional options you can edit the ClickOnce settings by selecting the Publish tab from the application's Properties page.

There is one problem with publishing a modular application using ClickOnce. The modules that are not referenced by the Shell application will not be deployed. Only the Shell assembly and its referenced assemblies will be deployed. Dynamically loaded modules won't be loaded unless the application manifest is modified.

Figure 8.5 presents the file structure that results after ClickOnce publishes an application. The root folder contains the deployment manifest. This file is used to determine the application version that will be installed. The root folder also contains a Setup.exe file. This is a bootstrapper file that contains all prerequisites that need to be installed before installing the application. The root folder also contains the application files. Each version of the application is inside its own folder.

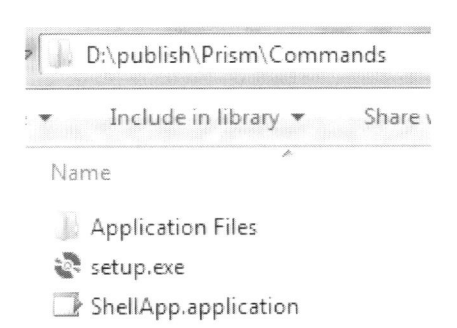

Figure 8.5 – *Publish folder structure for a ClickOnce deployment*

Each application specific folder contains the deployment manifest, the application manifest and the application files. These files have the .deploy extension in order to simplify server file mappings. This can be seen in figure 8.6.

The main problem with modifying an application manifest file and adding the remaining files is that the manifest contains hashes of the containing files. To be able to add the remaining assemblies we would need to modify the manifest and resign it. In order to help with this process the PRISM team released the ManifestManagerUtility tool. We can use this tool to add our missing files and resign the application.

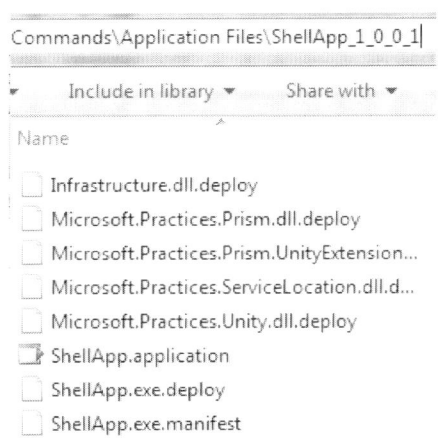

Figure 8.6 – *Application specific folder contents*

The ManifestManagerUtility uses the APIs exposed in the Microsoft.Build.Tasks.Deployment namespace. You can download the ManifestManagerUtility tool from the codeplex site at http://compositewpf.codeplex.com.

After you download the source you need to build it and use the resulting executable. To add the missing assemblies to the ClickOnce deployment open the MMU tool. Figure 8.7 presents the main UI.

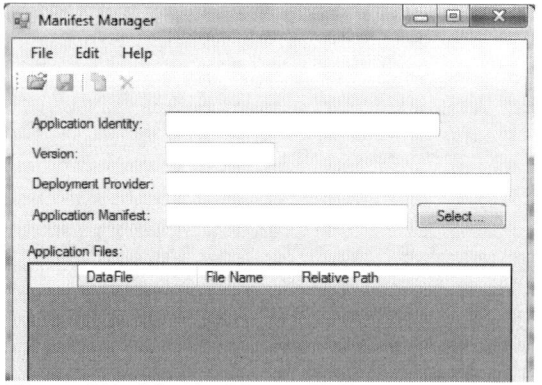

Figure 8.7 – *Manifest Manager Utility main user interface*

Click the open file toolbar button and navigate to the deployment manifest of your application. Once you select this file, the grid at the bottom of the interface will show you all the application files. This can be seen in figure 8.8.

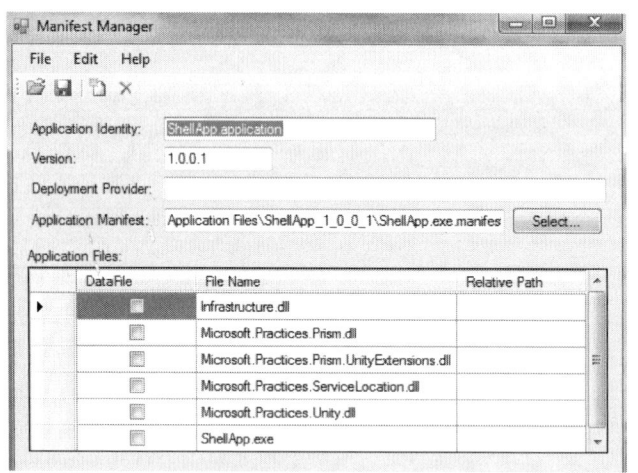

Figure 8.8 – *Manifest Manager Utility tool with imported deployment files*

The next step is to add the missing assemblies. Click the AddFile icon on the toolbar and select the module assembly. Once you do this a new dialog pops up that asks you to specify the relative path within the application directory. This can be seen in figure 8.9.

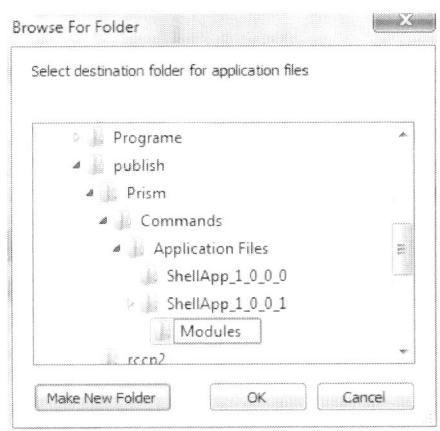

Figure 8.9 – Creating the folder for the missing module assemblies

Once you click OK, the selected files will be added to the list of existing files. This can be seen in figure 8.10.

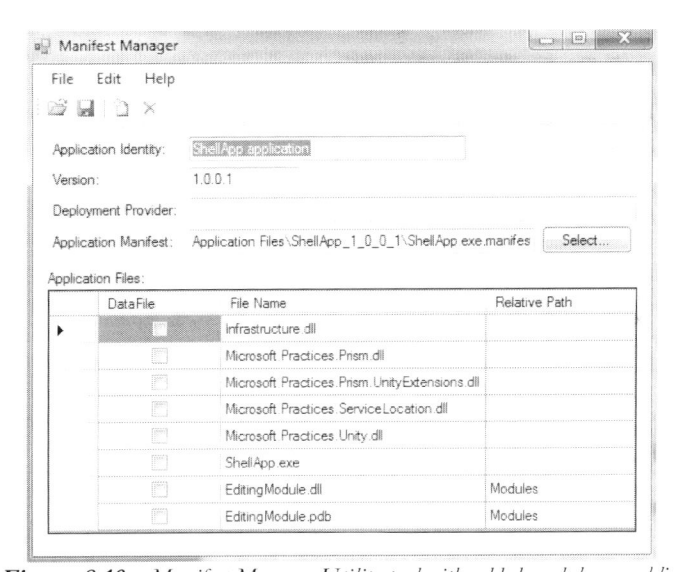

Figure 8.10 – Manifest Manager Utility tool with added module assemblies

The last step is to resign the application using the certificate and password you select. This can be seen in figure 8.11. Updating to a new version is done the same way.

8.2.2 Deploying WPF PRISM applications with WindowsInstaller

Windows Installer is a Windows feature that allows the user to install Windows Installer Packages. In order to create a package we need to create a Setup project in Visual Studio and add the files we want to deploy to this project. When the project is built, the Windows Installer Package file (an .msi file) is created. Creating Windows Installer Packages is no longer available in VisualStudio 2012. If you want to deploy using this option you will have to use an earlier version.

Figure 8.11 – *Manifest signing screen*

Using a Windows Installer Package allows us to make other modifications to the system besides copying the application files: add registry keys, install drivers and windows services and more. After installation, administrators can uninstall the application by using the Control Panel. The application can also be uninstalled by double clicking the .msi file again. This time the user will have 2 options: repair the install or remove it.

The major disadvantage of using a Windows installer package over Click Once is that automatic updates are not supported. If the application needs to check for updates it needs to use a custom solution. One such solution is to access a web service that returns the latest version available. The client can then check that version number against the installed version and show a link to the new version if the current version of the application is older. Setup projects can be configured to remove previous installations. This is done by checking the file version number. If you want to update a file all you have to do is change the version number and rebuild the Setup project. You can also add a menu item that calls the web service if you don't want to automatically call the update service at application startup.

Figure 8.12 – *Creating a new setup project in VS 2010*

Deploying with Windows Installer Packages has the same problem when it comes to PRISM applications that ClickOnce has: assemblies that have dynamically loaded modules are not added to the project output since there is no hard reference from the Shell project. To demonstrate how to deploy a PRISM application with Windows Installer we'll use the CompositeCommands sample application you built in a previous chapter.

Open the existing CompositeCommands solution and create a new Setup project. From the Add New Project dialog you select Other Projects-> Setup and Deployment->Setup Project. This can be seen in figure 8.12.

The next step is to add the ShellApp project output to the setup project. This will specify what files will be copied to the installation folder. Right-Click the Setup project in Solution Explorer and select Add Project Output. In the Add Project Output Group dialog select the ShellApp project from the projects list and select Primary Output. Figure 8.13 presents the selection.

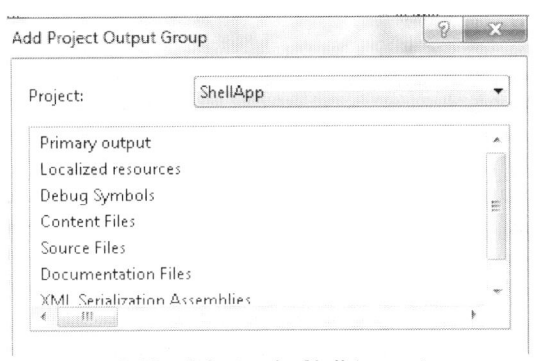

Figure 8.13 – *Selecting the ShellApp project output*

Selecting Application Folder in the File System tab should display the files that will be added. You can see, in figure 8.14, that we have the ShellApp output, as well as the referenced assemblies.

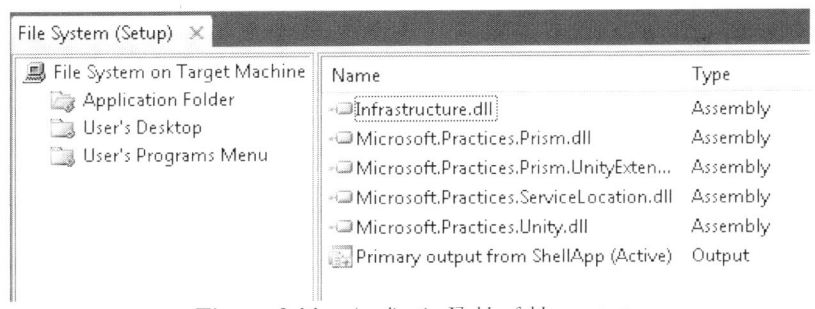

Figure 8.14 – *ApplicationFolder folder contents*

Our only problem is that the module assemblies will not be deployed. This is because the ShellApp project does not have a reference to the module assemblies. In order to fix this we'll add a Modules folder under the Application Folder, as figure 8.15 shows.

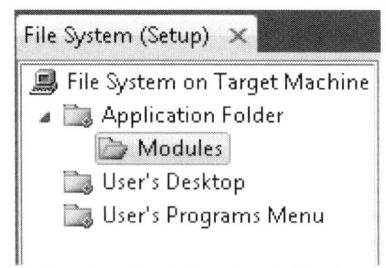

Figure 8.15 – *Creating the folder that holds the module assemblies*

After this we'll add a project output to the new Modules directory. Right click the Modules directory and select Add Project Output. Select the Primary Output option from the list, but this time select EditingModule as the project whose output will be deployed. This can be seen in figure 8.16.

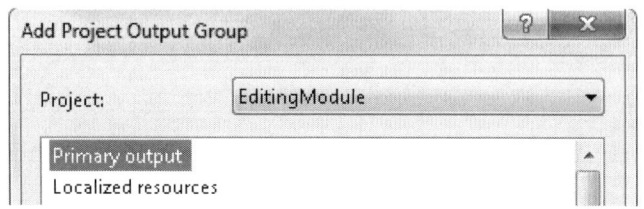

Figure 8.16 – *Selecting the project output for the EditingModule project*

Click Ok and the files will be displayed in the Modules folder as figure 8.17 shows.

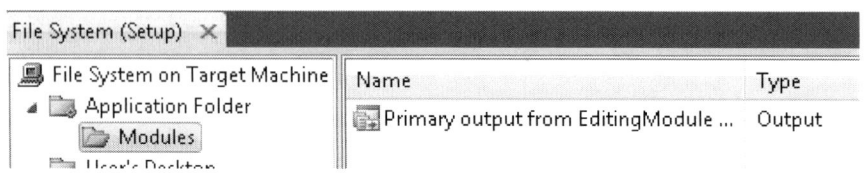

Figure 8.17 – *Modules folder contents*

In the Application Folder directory select the ShellApp output, right click it and choose to create a shortcut. Name the shortcut CompositeCommands. Figure 8.18 shows the shortcut that was created.

Figure 8.18 – *Creating a shortcut for the application*

Move the shortcut to the user's desktop folder as shown in figure 8.19.

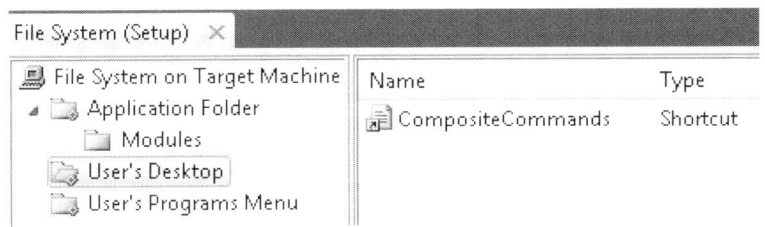

Figure 8.19 – Moving the shortcut to the desktop

The last step is to build the project and run the installer. After you run the installer you can see the shortcut that was added to the desktop. Clicking it will start the application.

8.2.3 Deploying WPF PRISM applications with WiX

Starting with Visual Studio 2012, the Setup project templates are no longer supported. In order to make a deployment using Windows Installer you have to use either a commercial product or the Windows Installer XML (WiX) toolset. You also have the option of using the InstallShield Limited Edition but this chapter will not cover this option.

The WiX toolset can be downloaded from http://wixtoolset.org. Using this toolset you can create and manage deployment projects. After you install the toolset, a few project templates will be added to Visual Studio. You can use these templates to create your setup projects. The following paragraphs describe how to deploy the same CompositeCommands sample we used in the previous section.

Open the composite commands solution, right click the solution and select the "add new project" option. From the Add New Project dialog, select the Windows Installer XML tab and then select the Setup Project template. This can be seen in figure 8.20.

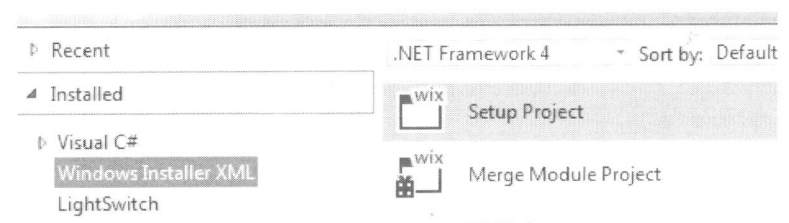

Figure 8.20 – Creating a new WiX Setup project

After the project is created, the main project file will be opened in Visual Studio. This is an XML file that will be used to configure the setup project. We need to add references to the assemblies we need to deploy. Right click the References folder in the setup project and select the Add Reference option. From the dialog, select the Projects tab and add each available project. This can be seen in figure 8.21.

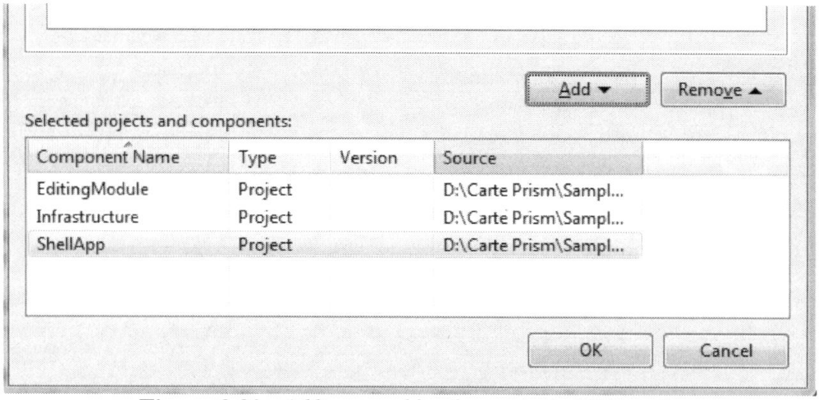

Figure 8.21 - *Adding assembly references to the WiX project*

In the project XML file, edit the Feature tag inside the Product tag as shown in listing 8.3.

Listing 8.3 – *Defining the component group references*
```
<Feature Id="ProductFeature" Title="SetupProject" Level="1">
    <ComponentGroupRef Id="ProductComponents" />
    <ComponentGroupRef Id="ProductModules" />
</Feature>
```

This defines component group references for two component groups that will be defined later in the file. These groups will contain the files that need to be deployed. Edit the first Fragment tag as shown in listing 8.4.

Listing 8.4 – *Specifying the deployment directory structure*
```
<Fragment>
  <Directory Id="TARGETDIR" Name="SourceDir">
    <Directory Id="ProgramFilesFolder">
      <Directory Id="INSTALLFOLDER"
                 Name="CompositeCommandSample" >
         <Directory Id="MODULES" Name="Modules" />
      </Directory>
    </Directory>
  </Directory>
</Fragment>
```

This Fragment tag specifies the directory structure where the application files will be copied. The application will be copied in the "c:\Program Files\CompositeCommandSample" directory. You can also notice that we added the Modules directory inside the CompositeCommandSample directory. This is where the module assemblies will be copied.

In the last Fragment tag we'll have two ComponentGroup tags. These are the tags for which we defined the references earlier. The first ComponentGroup tag will contain the Shell and Infrastructure assemblies as well as the shared PRISM assemblies. The second ComponentGroup tag will be used to add the module assembly. Add the first ComponentGroup tag as shown in listing 8.5.

Listing 8.5 – *Specifying the Shell, Infrastructure and PRISM assemblies deployment location*
```xml
<ComponentGroup Id="ProductComponents" Directory="INSTALLFOLDER">
  <Component Guid="9AF0A15B-C8D9-4208-B477-A0E12AB6377D">
    <File Source="$(var.ShellApp.TargetPath)" KeyPath="yes"/>
  </Component>
  <Component Guid="34F...">
    <File Source="$(var.Infrastructure.TargetPath)"
        KeyPath="yes"/>
  </Component>
  <Component Guid="5B0...">
    <File Source="C:\Program Files\Prism41\Bin\Desktop\Microsoft.Practices.Prism.dll"
        KeyPath="yes"/>
  </Component>
  <Component Guid="0F9...">
    <File Source="C:\Program Files\Prism41\Bin\Desktop\Microsoft.Practices.Unity.dll"
        KeyPath="yes"/>
  </Component>
  <Component Guid="0BD...">
    <File Source="C:\Program Files\Prism41\Bin\Desktop\Microsoft.Practices.ServiceLocation.dll" KeyPath="yes"/>
  </Component>
  <Component Guid="A43...">
    <File Source="C:\Program Files\Prism41\Bin\Desktop\Microsoft.Practices.Prism.UnityExtensions.dll" KeyPath="yes"/>
  </Component>
</ComponentGroup>
```

The ComponentGroup tag contains some Component tags. These tags define the files that need to be added. Most of the Guid values are incomplete but you can generate the component Guid values by using the Visual Studio Create Guid feature from the Tools menu. Each Component tag contains a File tag. The Source attribute specifies the name of the file that will be copied to the destination folder. You can see that the first 2 files use variables to specify the file location. This is possible only because we added the project references at the beginning.

Add the second ComponentGroup tag as shown in listing 8.6. This tag specifies where the module assemblies should be copied as well as their location. Since we have a project reference, we can use a variable name to specify the source file location.

Listing 8.6 – *Specifying the module assembly deployment location*
```xml
<ComponentGroup Id="ProductModules" Directory="MODULES">
  <Component Guid="0BA9CB98-4FBD-4CBE-B19C-27B683957366">
    <File Source="$(var.EditingModule.TargetPath)" KeyPath="yes"/>
  </Component>
</ComponentGroup>
```

Everything is ready to be built now. Build the projects and go to the build output folder for the setup project. You should see the install file.

8.3 Summary
This chapter presented some of the options we have when deploying a PRISM application. Silverlight

applications are the easiest to deploy since all we need to do is copy the xap files to the correct location. After this we looked at deploying WPF applications. We have 3 options here: deploy using ClickOnce, using the WindowsInstaller and using WiX.

One inconvenient when deploying WPF PRISM applications is that modules that are not referenced by the main application will not be included in the deployment by default. We have to explicitly add those assemblies to the final package. When deploying with ClickOnce we can use the Manifest Manager Utility tool. Using this tool also allows us to resign the application manifest file.

Deploying WPF applications with WindowsInstaller is no longer supported as of VisualStudio 2012. One free available solution is to use WiX. In these cases we can manually add the module assemblies to the installation folder.

REFERENCES

Brumfield, Bob; Cox, Geoff; Hill David; et al. "Developer's Guide to Microsoft PRISM 4". Microsoft Press, March 2011

Noyes, Brian. "Working with PRISM 4". SilverlightShow, April 2012

Seemann, Mark. "Dependency Injection in .NET". Manning Publications, September 2011

Block, Glenn. "Managed Extensibility Framework: Building Composable Apps in .NET 4 with the Managed Extensibility Framework". MSDN Magazine, February 2010

Smith, Josh. "Patterns: WPF Apps with the Model-View-ViewModel Design Pattern", MSDN Magazine, February 2009

Gamma, Erich, et al. "Design Patterns. Elements of Reusable Object-Oriented Software". Addison-Wesley, November 1994

Bishop, Judith. "C# 3.0 Design Patterns". O'Reilly Media, January 2008

Betts, Dominic, et al. "Dependency Injection with Unity". Microsoft Press, August 2013

APPENDIX: THE PRISM FRAMEWORK

Installing PRISM
The Microsoft PRISM Framework is currently at version 4.1. The 4.1 version of the framework supports Silverlight 5 and .NET 4.0 and is available from the codeplex site at compositewpf.codeplex.com. From here you can go to the Downloads tab and select the version you want to download. After you run the executable you will need to choose the disk location where you want to install the files.

After the installation, the library files are not registered with Visual Studio. This means that you cannot add references to the PRISM assemblies, from the Add References dialog box, without using the browse option. In order to register the PRISM assemblies you can use the RegisterPrismBinaries.bat batch file. To unregister the assemblies use the same batch file with the /u option.

PRISM assemblies
The PRISM binaries are split into 3 folders representing the 3 technologies that can use PRISM: desktop, Silverlight and Windows Phone. PRISM for desktop contains 4 assemblies. The content for each of these assemblies is presented in the following paragraphs.

The Microsoft.Practices.Prism.dll assembly is the main PRISM assembly. It contains types that allow you to implement modular applications, UI composition via regions, region navigation and others. This assembly contains types that allow you to communicate in a loosely coupled manner by using event aggregation and composite commands. The assembly also contains types that allow you to develop MVVM applications more easily.

The Microsoft.Practices.Prism.Interactivity.dll assembly contains types that help with user interaction in the context of building MVVM applications. This assembly contains types that implement the interaction request pattern. With this pattern, the view-model triggers an event in order to request an interaction. The view subscribes to this event by using an event trigger and displays the interaction window. The Silverlight version of this assembly also contains some trigger actions that allow the developer to present the interaction windows.

The Microsoft.Practices.Prism.UnityExtensions.dll assembly contains types that allow you to use the UnityContainer with the PRISM library. More exactly, the assembly contains a Unity specific bootstrapper as well as a service locator implementation that delegates all the work to a UnityContainer instance.

The Microsoft.Practices.Prism.MefExtensions.dll assembly contains types that allow you to use the PRISM library with MEF. More exactly, the assembly contains a MEF specific bootstrapper as well as a service locator implementation that delegates all the work to a CompositionContainer instance. The assembly also contains types that allow you to use event aggregation, UI composition and modularity with MEF.

Source code

The PrismLibrary folder contains the PRISM library source code. Each version appears in its own folder. You can open the solution files in Visual Studio in order to further inspect how the library works. This is a necessary step if you want to extend the framework at some point.

Quickstarts and reference implementations

The installed files also contain sample applications for each of the PRISM features. These samples can be found in the Quickstarts folder. You can find samples for: MVVM, commanding, event aggregation, modularity, ui composition, state-based navigation, view-switching navigation and multi targeting.

The install folder also contains 2 reference implementations. These are more complex applications that use various PRISM features. The MVVM RI reference implementation presents how to implement the MVVM pattern, including user interactions, in a Silverlight application. The StockTrader RI reference implementation presents most of the PRISM features in the form of a stock trader application. The application showcases how to use modularity, UI composition, region navigation as well as event aggregation.

Printed in Great Britain
by Amazon.co.uk, Ltd.,
Marston Gate.